HUNTER – GATHERER
FORAGING

FIVE SIMPLE MODELS

HUNTER – GATHERER
FORAGING
FIVE SIMPLE MODELS

ROBERT L. BETTINGER
University of California, Davis
Davis, California

ELIOT WERNER PUBLICATIONS, INC.
CLINTON CORNERS, NEW YORK

Library of Congress Cataloging-in-Publication Data

Bettinger, Robert L.
  Hunter-gatherer foraging : five simple models / Robert L. Bettinger.
    p. cm.
  Includes bibliographical references.
  ISBN 978-0-9797731-3-6 (pbk.)
  1. Hunting and gathering societies—Statistical methods. I. Title.
GN388.B48 2009
306.3'640727—dc22

2009012293

ISBN-10: 0-9797731-3-X
ISBN-13: 978-0-9797731-3-6

Copyright © 2009 Eliot Werner Publications, Inc.
PO Box 268, Clinton Corners, New York 12514
http://www.eliotwerner.com

Printed in the United States of America

Many contributed to this book, but none more than my
good friend Lisa Deitz — to whom it is dedicated

PREFACE

This is a primer on foraging models relevant to the study of hunter-gatherers. It is intended for students new to the subject matter—especially those with little mathematical training and similarly challenged ethnographers, ethnologists, and archaeologists who are familiar with the principles of foraging theory but have never mastered any of its individual models. There are more of them than one might think. The diet breadth model is the backbone of hunter-gatherer foraging research, for example, but I would wager that of the many scholars who have referred to it in print or applied its logic to interpret their data, fewer than one in ten has ever worked through a diet breadth problem with real numbers. I doubt the others are lazy: it is simply that no existing source provides instructions for calculating diet breadth. As my colleague Bruce Winterhalder likes to point out, the biological types have presented several quite similar but not exactly identical variations of the diet breadth model that codify slightly different assumptions by means of formulas that are correct but generally incomplete, failing to specify all the operations required for a solution. Winterhalder has mastered these complexities, but too many without his considerable mathematical skills give up without even trying, convinced that the best they can do is gather the gist of the diet breadth model and use its more intuitively obvious implications to help them think about hunter-gatherer behavior.

This is unsatisfactory for several reasons, not the least of which is that it makes foraging theory seem at once more simple and more complicated than it really is—so simple that the math doesn't matter, so complicated that only the mathematically gifted can really do it. Neither is true: the math does matter and is simple enough that anyone who mastered elementary high school algebra can do it. The math matters because, to draw an analogy with cooking, reading the recipe is not the same as cooking the dish. One cannot really know how any foraging model works (i.e., what it does) without actually performing the mathematical operations needed to solve a specific problem. The models presented here are so simple that this is easily done; anyone sufficiently inclined can work through a whole battery of problems and in this way come to understand the relationship between data input and model output—that is, how much the data must change to produce a fundamentally different outcome. The minimal computation required can be done with pencil and paper or hand calculator, but most efficiently on a computer.

I do virtually all my statistical and quantitative work using Microsoft® Excel and strongly recommend using that (or a similar spreadsheet application) to program the equations presented here. As far as I am aware, there are no commercial or freeware applications for most of these models, and I ultimately rejected the idea of providing a CD with my versions because doing so would deprive readers of a valuable learning experience. There is no substitute for developing your own spreadsheet treatments: you will know exactly what went into them and exactly how they work.

Since we're on this subject, it is worth noting that while these models are simple, they are very powerful precisely because of that. They argue that human foraging behavior can be explained with reference to the interaction between a few important variables. While these models oversimplify the real world, they are surely the right place to start when attempting to understand it. They make straightforward, relatively easy-to-test predictions. Complex models, on the other hand, make complex predictions that are correspondingly more difficult to test. This difference is crucial in archaeology, where taphonomic and other processes continually degrade the resolution of the material record—hence our ability to assess the kind of fine-grained test implications that complex models typically generate. I have never felt the need to apologize for using simple models to explain human behavior, nor should the reader. After all, isn't this what science is supposed to be about: making the world simpler and easier to understand?

A word of caution is in order. Because this primer is designed for readers with limited mathematical background and experience with quantitative modeling, I have consistently opted for clarity in presentation and explication of formulas and data, sometimes at variance with accepted conventions. Results are sometimes expressed to more significant digits than would normally be warranted, for example, because it has been my experience that this makes it easier for students to check their work (and more rewarding when the numbers actually match!). For this reason, while my purpose in writing this primer is to encourage its readers to pursue research using these models and present their results to professional audiences at scholarly meetings or in published form, this primer should not be used as a style guide. I strongly urge readers to run all their work by a knowledgeable reviewer who is willing to take the time to check their math and the form in which it is presented, a practice that is standard even among experts, who are as mistake-prone as anyone else. As my colleague Donald Grayson quips, "We have friends check our work to keep the rest of the world from finding out how stupid we really are." While I followed that advice here, having others double-check my work for errors, I am naturally responsible for any that remain.

This is where I thank people who contributed to this primer. Among all these individuals, Lisa Deitz certainly ranks first, having read several versions of the manuscript, checking them for grammar, logic, and computational accuracy and making me look smarter than I really am. I am equally indebted to my editor and publisher Eliot Werner, who helped me get my first book into print almost two decades ago and was foolish enough to undertake this project. In a world filled with outrageously priced books, Eliot is one of a rare few individuals dedicated to publishing good books at a reasonable price — we worked hard to keep the price down on this one. Thanks are also due to Bruce Winterhalder, who read an early draft of the manuscript and encouraged me to get it into print; and two anonymous reviewers who, on the basis of reading this same early draft, urged Eliot to go ahead with getting a more polished version of it published.

CONTENTS

HUNTER–GATHERER FORAGING

FIVE SIMPLE MODELS

CHAPTER 1

HOW TO CALCULATE OPTIMAL DIET BREADTH

BOTSWANA–NAMIBIA BORDER, Dobe area. A !Kung hunter comes across the tracks of a duiker (*Cephalophus* sp.). The tracks look fresh, indicating the prey is relatively close: a short stalk, single close-range arrow shot, and brief pursuit of the wounded prey would take two hours at most. Duiker average something like 20 kilograms so this would be a reasonable kill. However, earlier the hunter encountered older tracks and other signs suggesting there are a fair number of warthog (*Phacochoerus africanus*) somewhere nearby. Warthog are much larger than duiker (ca. 80 kilograms) and would be a much better kill if the hunter can locate one, which he's reasonably certain he can with a few more hours of searching. The hunter then has to decide which is his best choice, the small package duiker (which can be had in relatively short order) or the bigger package warthog (which will take substantially longer). The *diet breadth model* is designed to address such problems.

INTRODUCTION

Diet breadth is perhaps the simplest of the optimal foraging models. It belongs to the family of "contingency models," all of which configure the problem to be solved as an instant in time that presents two courses of action demanding an immediate choice. The diet breadth model envisions a forager working in an environment with several different prey types — some large, some small, some fast, some slow. The contingency is an encounter with one of these; the courses of action are "Catch it and eat it" or "Ignore it and seek something better" and the rational decision is the one that produces the higher expected rate of return. Generally return is calculated in kcal (kilocalories or just calories) per unit of time, although the model can take any other benefit/cost form we want. The benefit, for example, could as easily be in units of "flavor" or "prestige," and cost in U.S. dollars.

The crux of the diet breadth model is the dividing of foraging into two components, search and handling. Search is the part of foraging given to

1

finding prey. Thus *search time* is simply the time it takes to locate a prey type—its encounter time, whether the encounter is direct (I see it) or indirect (I sense it or see its tracks). Handling entails all the steps needed to consume a prey type after it is found. Thus *handling time* is the amount of time it takes to acquire (e.g., stalk and slay) an item and ready it for consumption (some animal behaviorists extend this to include digestion time, the amount of time it takes for the item to pass through the gut). Handling time is sometimes referred to as *post-encounter* time. The trick is to come up with a mixture of prey types that minimize the combination of search and handling time per unit of energetic return. The best prey produce many kcal per unit of handling time once found, but if they are very hard to find (search time is high), foraging just for them may produce low returns for foraging time (search time + handling time). If we add lower quality prey, search time will go down but handling time will go up because by definition lower ranking prey produce fewer kcal per unit of handling time.

In Figure 1.1, for example, foraging time initially decreases as diet breadth increases because search time decreases faster than handling time increases. As diet breadth continues to widen, however, the decrease in

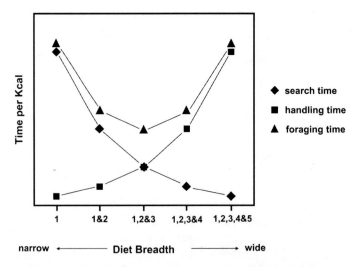

Figure 1.1. Effect of decreasing prey selectivity (increasing diet breadth) on search time, handling time, and foraging time (search time + handling time). Prey types (1, 2, 3, 4, and 5) are ranked from highest to lowest, left to right, by kcal per unit of handling time and enter the diet in order of rank so that handling time always increases as lower ranking prey are added (diet breadth widens). Search time always decreases because widening diet breadth means more kinds of prey are taken when encountered: less prey selectivity means lower search time. The optimal solution minimizes foraging time per kcal and thus maximizes kcal per unit of foraging time.

search time is eventually overtaken by the increase in handling time, causing foraging time to rise again. In this case optimal diet breadth is squarely in the center of Figure 1.1, where foraging time (search time + handling time) per kcal has dropped to its lowest level, thus maximizing kcal obtained per unit of foraging time.

THE MODEL

In the following example, there are three resources—mice, deer, and rabbit—whose critical characteristics are given in Table 1.1.

Table 1.1. Prey Characteristics

	Mice	Deer	Rabbit
Kcal per item	25 kcal	100 kcal	75 kcal
Search time per item	1 min	6 min	2 min
Handling time per item	2 min	3 min	5 min

These kcal values and search and handling times are unrealistic (the edible parts of a real mule deer add up to perhaps 100,000 kcal, for example, and for an average black-tailed jackrabbit about 3500 kcal). More importantly they are small, which is intentional. Small values demystify the math, making it less daunting to the uninitiated. (For some reason most people find it easier to think about dividing 100 by 6 than dividing 100,000 by 6000). The point is not to capture a real-world situation; the point is to illustrate how the diet breadth model works in the simplest possible way, and especially how it balances energy and time to maximize energy per unit of time. Once you understand how the model works, it will be easy to plug in more realistic values and solve problems with real-world implications. That said, let's calculate the optimal diet breadth for our three resources.

Step 1: Rank prey by handling return rate (kcal/handling time). The 1st ranked prey will always be in the diet.

The first step is to rank different prey according to units of energy (kcal) per unit of handling time. Easy. Just divide energy (kcal) of each prey type by its handling time and rank prey types in descending order from highest kcal/handling time to lowest kcal/handling time. This is tantamount to ranking prey types in order of preference, from the one you'd most like to encounter (highest kcal payoff per unit of handling time) to the one you'd least like to encounter (smallest kcal payoff per unit of handling time). Handling time is just as important as kcal value here because to use a prey type requires its handling (e.g., stalking, butchering, cooking, etc.).

Accordingly, if its handling time is low enough, a prey type with few kcal may be more highly ranked than a prey type with many more kcal but a proportionally higher handling time. Note also that while I use the term "prey" throughout, and our prey here are all vertebrates (mice, deer, and rabbit), the reference is really to a resource type that could as easily be a plant as an animal.

Table 1.2. Ranking of Prey by Kcal per Unit of Handling Time

	Mice	Deer	Rabbit
Kcal per item	25 kcal	100 kcal	75 kcal
Handling time per item	2 min	3 min	5 min
Kcal/handling time	12.50 kcal/min	33.33 kcal/min	15.00 kcal/min
Rank:	3rd	1st	2nd

Table 1.2 makes it clear that deer is 1st ranked at 33.33 kcal/min, followed by rabbit (15.00 kcal/min) and mice (12.50 kcal/min). Now rearrange Table 1.2, ranking from highest to lowest, left to right, placing deer at the left, rabbit in the middle, and mice at the right (as shown in Table 1.3). This ranking implies that deer on the left will always be on our foraging menu. We will always stop and take a deer whenever we encounter one because it's the highest ranked. Having found a deer, it will *never* make sense to go on searching for something better: deer is as good as it gets.

Table 1.3. Prey Ordered by Rank

	Deer	Rabbit	Mice
Kcal per item	100 kcal	75 kcal	25 kcal
Search time per item	6 min	2 min	1 min
Handling time per item	3 min	5 min	2 min
Kcal/handling time	33.33 kcal/min	15.00 kcal/min	12.50 kcal/min
Rank:	1st	2nd	3rd

Step 2: Determine whether the 2nd ranked prey should be in the diet by comparing its handling return rate (kcal/handling time) to the foraging return rate (kcal/search+handling time) for a diet that includes only the 1st ranked prey. This will further entail Steps 3 and 4.

Okay, we should eat deer, but the next question is "Should we eat rabbit, which is 2nd ranked?" That is, if we chance upon a rabbit while searching, should we catch and eat the rabbit or should we pass on the rabbit and go on searching for deer? This is a contingency (we have chanced upon a rabbit) and the question ("Should we eat it?") is easily answered. We just ask whether the calories (kcal) gained per unit of *just the handling time* for the rabbit is greater than the calories gained per unit of *search plus handling* time for the deer. This is sensible, for in the logic of the contingency just posed, we have already located the rabbit so no search time is needed. The deer, however, must be searched for and, once found, handled. To answer this question, we have to back up a minute and calculate our foraging return rate when we only eat (search for and handle) deer.

Step 3: Calculate the foraging return rate (kcal/search+handling time) for a diet that includes only the 1st ranked prey.

This is easily done from the data given in Table 1.3. It takes 6 minutes to find a deer and another 3 minutes to get it ready to eat, from which we benefit 100 kcal, so the overall rate of return when foraging exclusively for deer is 11.11 kcal/min (Table 1.4). *100/9 = 11.11*

Table 1.4. Foraging Return Rate for a Diet Including Only Deer (1st Ranked)

	Deer only
Kcal per item	100 kcal
Search time per item	6 min
Handling time per item	3 min
= Foraging time per item	= 9 min
Kcal/foraging time:	11.11 kcal/min

Step 4: If the handling return rate (kcal/handling time) for the 2nd ranked prey is greater than or equal to the foraging return rate (kcal/search+handling time) for a diet that includes only the 1st ranked prey, the 2nd ranked prey should be added to the diet. If not, it should not.

This is easy because we already know the handling return rate for rabbit, having calculated it in Step 1 to obtain our initial rankings (Table 1.3). If we stop to bag the rabbit, we expect to gain 15.00 kcal/min. If we continue to search for deer, we expect to gain 11.11 kcal/min (Table 1.4). Since 15.00 kcal/min is greater than 11.11 kcal/min, obviously we should bag and eat the rabbit, which means our diet will include both deer and rabbit (Table 1.5).

Step 5: Determine whether the 3rd ranked prey should be in the diet by comparing its handling return rate (kcal/handling time) to the foraging return rate (kcal/search+handling time) for a diet that includes only the 1st and 2nd ranked prey. This will further entail Steps 6–12.

Table 1.5. Handling Return Rate for Rabbit (2nd Ranked) versus Foraging Return Rate for a Diet Including Only Deer (1st Ranked)

	Deer only	Rabbit
Kcal per item	100 kcal	75 kcal
Search time per item	6 min	
Handling time per item	3 min	5 min
= Foraging time per item	= 9 min	
Kcal/ foraging time:	11.11kcal/min	Kcal/ handling time: 15.00 kcal/min

The next question is obviously "What about mice, which are 3rd ranked? Should we eat them?" Here things get a little tricky because again we have to back up and calculate our overall rate of energetic return (foraging return rate) when we eat *both* deer and rabbit (and only deer and rabbit). This is important because, as with the rabbit earlier, we are faced with a contingency. We have chanced upon a mouse. Should we eat it or continue looking for deer and rabbit? To decide, we need to know the foraging return rate for deer&rabbit, the rate we would obtain by passing on the mouse and continuing to search for deer and rabbit, which we will have to handle once we find them. Then we can compare that foraging rate with the handling return rate for mice, the rate we would obtain by catching and eating the mouse we have already found. The calculations are a little fussy but quite simple if we proceed logically.

Step 6: Determine the proportional contribution of the 1st and 2nd ranked prey to a diet that includes only the 1st and 2nd ranked prey.

The first thing we need to figure out is in what proportion we eat rabbit and deer when only deer and rabbit are in the diet. By what is known as the "zero-one rule," items that are in the diet are *always* pursued and handled when encountered; conversely things not in the diet are *never* pursed or handled when encountered. This means we will eat rabbit and deer in the proportion in which they are encountered. The key point to understand here is that frequency of encounter will be inversely proportional to search time. This makes perfect sense. Large search time means few encounters; small search time means many encounters. In this case search time is 6 minutes for deer and 2 minutes for rabbit. Items per minute is exactly the inverse—1 item per 6 minutes for deer and 1 item per 2 minutes for rabbit, as shown in Table 1.6.

To get the overall encounter rate, the total number of items (deer and rabbit) encountered per minute, we simply add these individual

Table 1.6. Proportional Contribution of Deer and Rabbit to a Diet Including Only Deer and Rabbit (1st and 2nd Ranked)

	Deer	Rabbit	Deer&rabbit
Search time per item	6 min	2 min	
Items per search time	1/6 min	1/2 min	
Items per min	.17	.50	.67
Proportional contribution:	.17/.67 = .25	.50/.67 = .75	

encounter rates. In this case .17 deer per minute plus .50 rabbits per minute equals .67 deer&rabbit per minute. The proportional contribution of deer to the deer&rabbit diet is the fraction that deer contribute to this total encounter rate, or .17 / .67 = .25. Correspondingly the proportional contribution of rabbit is .50 / .67 = .75.

Step 7: Determine kcal per item for a diet that includes only the 1st and 2nd ranked prey.

The next thing we need to know is kcal per item in the mixed deer&rabbit diet. The thing to keep in mind here is what "item" means. According to the proportional contribution values just calculated in Step 6, it means a creature that is one time out of four a deer and three times out of four a rabbit. This makes sense. We encounter 2 deer for every 6 rabbits, so when we encounter an item on our menu (which includes both deer and rabbit), 25% of the time it is a deer (100 kcal) and 75% of the time it is a rabbit (75 kcal). Thus the kcal per item in the mixed deer&rabbit diet is just the kcal value of deer (100 kcal) times their proportional contribution (.25) plus the kcal value of rabbit (75 kcal) times their proportional contribution (.75), or (100 kcal x .25) + (75 kcal x .75) = 81.25 kcal/item (Table 1.7). Again, easy.

Table 1.7. Kcal per Item for a Diet Including Only Deer and Rabbit (1st and 2nd Ranked)

	Deer	Rabbit	Deer&rabbit
Kcal per item	100 kcal	75 kcal	81.25 kcal
Proportional contribution	.25	.75	
Proportional contribution x kcal per item	25.00 kcal	56.25 kcal	

Step 8: Determine handling time per item for a diet that includes only the 1st and 2nd ranked prey.

Now we must determine the handling time per item for our deer&rabbit foraging mix. This is easily calculated because we know the handling times for deer and rabbit (Step 1) *and* we also know their proportional contribution in the deer&rabbit diet (Step 6). The handling time per item for this mixed diet is just the handling time for deer (3 minutes) times the proportional contribution of deer (.25) plus the handling time for rabbit (5 minutes) times the proportional contribution of rabbit (.75). So handling for deer (3 min x .25 = .75 min) plus handling for rabbit (5 min x .75 = 3.75 min) gives .75 min + 3.75 min = 4.50 min (Table 1.8). Easy.

Table 1.8. Handling Time per Item for a Diet Including Only Deer and Rabbit (1st and 2nd Ranked)

	Deer	Rabbit	Deer&rabbit
Proportional contribution	.25	.75	
Handling time per item	3 min	5 min	4.50 min
Proportional contribution x handling time	.75 min	3.75 min	

Step 9: Determine search time per item for a diet that includes only the 1st and 2nd ranked prey.

Next we need to determine search time per item when we hunt for rabbit and deer at the same time (diet breadth includes only deer and rabbit). Again, this is simple because we know that search time and encounter rate are inversely related, and we've already calculated the rate at which one encounters either a deer or a rabbit, which came to .67 deer&rabbit per minute (Table 1.6). So the search time for deer&rabbit (the amount of time it takes to locate either a deer or a rabbit) is the inverse of their joint encounter rate, or 1 / .67 min = 1.50 min (note rounding error). More generally, to determine search time when two or more items are in the diet, first compute for each item the inverse of its search time as a decimal fraction (as we did here for deer and again for rabbit), add these individual encounter rates, and compute the inverse of their sum. Proportional contribution can be calculated from the individual encounter rates, as in Step 6. Note that, as we would expect, it takes less time to find either a deer or a rabbit than it takes to find either one individually (Table 1.9).

Step 10: Determine foraging time per item for a diet that includes only the 1st and 2nd ranked prey.

We can now calculate the foraging time per item (search time plus handling time) for the deer&rabbit diet (Table 1.10).

Table 1.9. Search Time per Item for a Diet Including Only Deer and Rabbit (1st and 2nd Ranked)

	Deer	Rabbit	Deer&rabbit
Search time per item	6 min	2 min	1.50 min
Encounter rate	1/6 min	1/2 min	
Items per min	.17	.50	0.67

Step 11: Calculate the foraging return rate (kcal / search+handling time) for a diet that includes only the 1st and 2nd ranked prey.

The rest is easier still. To calculate the foraging return rate for the deer&rabbit diet, just divide kcal per item (Table 1.7) by foraging time per item (Table 1.10). The result is shown in Table 1.11, along with the formerly obtained foraging return rate for the deer-only diet (Table 1.4).

As expected, the overall rate of return for deer&rabbit (13.54 kcal/min) is higher than the overall rate of return for deer alone (11.11 kcal/min). We gain more calories when we eat both deer and rabbit than when we eat just deer. We suffer a decrease in kcal per item (18.75 kcal/item) and a small increase in handling time (1.50 minutes) but obtain a large decrease in search time (4.50 minutes), resulting in a net increase in the rate at which we obtain calories. Note that if rabbit had fewer calories, kcal per item might have decreased so much that adding rabbit to the diet might not have made sense. That's why we do the math! This point is illustrated in the next step, where we consider adding mice to our deer&rabbit diet.

Step 12: If the handling return rate (kcal / handling time) for the 3rd ranked prey is greater than or equal to foraging return rate (kcal / search+handling time) for a diet that includes only the 1st and 2nd ranked prey, the 3rd ranked prey should be added to the diet. If not, it should not.

This last step answers the question we raised in Step 5: "Should mice be added to the mixed deer&rabbit diet?" The decision is rather simple. As before, we ask if we chance on a mouse in the course of foraging for deer

Table 1.10. Foraging Time per Item for a Diet Including Only Deer and Rabbit (1st and 2nd Ranked)

	Deer&rabbit
Search time per item	1.50 min
Handling time per item	4.50 min
= Foraging time per item:	= 6.00 min

Table 1.11. Foraging Return Rate for a Diet Including Only Deer (1st Ranked) versus a Diet Including Only Deer and Rabbit (1st and 2nd Ranked)

	Deer only	Deer&rabbit
Kcal per item	100.00 kcal	81.25 kcal
Search time per item	6.00 min	1.50 min
Handling time per item	3.00 min	4.50 min
= Foraging time per item	= 9.00 min	= 6.00 min
Kcal/foraging time:	11.11 kcal/min	13.54 kcal/min

and rabbit, "Should we catch it and eat it?" Note here that mice are very common. Since search time for mice is 1 minute, while that for deer is 6 minutes, for rabbit 2 minutes, and for deer&rabbit 1.50 minutes, it might seem reasonable to eat mice—for in this way we would save a lot of search time.

What is at issue here, however, is not the commonness of mice, for the question we are asking has nothing to do with commonness. The question is "If we chance upon one, should we eat it?" As the contingency is posed, we've already located a mouse, so its search time is not in question— we've already found it! What we want to know is if we bag and eat the mouse, what is the rate of caloric gain? Is it greater than the overall rate of return we would obtain by passing on the mouse and continuing our search for deer&rabbit? So the question is simple.

From Step 11 we know that the overall rate of energetic return (foraging return rate) for deer&rabbit = 13.54 kcal/min. We also know from Step 1 (Table 1.3) that the handling return rate for mice = 25 kcal per mouse divided by 2 minutes handling time per mouse = 12.50 kcal/min. Thus if we stop to eat the mouse, we expect to gain 12.50 kcal/min, which is less than if we pass on the mouse and continue to search for deer&rabbit—from which we expect to gain 13.54 kcal/min (Table 1.12). Here's our answer: "Don't eat mice!"

In this case adding mice to the diet would decrease search time per item (broadening diet *always* decreases search time per item). Further, because mice are so quickly handled and so common, it would also decrease handling time per item (in contrast to adding rabbit, which increased handling time). However, mice are so small (contain so few kcal) that adding them to the diet would increase foraging time per kcal.

In this example there were only 3 prey types and the handling rate for the 3rd ranked prey was too low to warrant including it in the diet. This would have been sufficient to exclude still lower ranking prey (had there been any) from the diet without further calculation. That is, calculation of optimal diet stops when one reaches the first prey type whose handling

Table 1.12. Handling Return Rate for Mice (3rd Ranked) versus Foraging Return Rate for a Diet Including Only Deer and Rabbit (1st and 2nd Ranked)

	Deer&rabbit	Mice
Kcal per item	81.25 kcal	25 kcal
Search time per item	1.50 min	
Handling time per item	4.50 min	2.00 min
= Foraging time per item	= 6.00 min	
Kcal/		Kcal/
foraging time:	13.54 kcal/min	handling time: 12.50 kcal/min

return rate is too low to justify inclusion in the diet; any lower ranking prey will obviously also be excluded. Had the handling rate for the 3rd ranked prey been large enough to warrant inclusion in the diet ($\geq$ 13.54 kcal/min handling), and had there been still lower ranking prey, the question would then have shifted to ask whether a 4th ranked prey should be included in the diet. In that event Steps 5–12 would be repeated, changed only to reflect the inclusion of the 3rd ranked prey in the diet and the possibility of adding the 4th. For example, Step 5 would now read, "Determine whether the 4th ranked prey should be in the diet by comparing its handling return rate (kcal/handling time) to the foraging return rate (kcal/search+handling time) for a diet that includes only the 1st, 2nd, and 3rd ranked prey."

Since the handling return rate for the 4th ranked prey would already be known from Step 1, this would merely require calculating the foraging return rate for a diet that includes only the 1st, 2nd, and 3rd ranked prey, beginning with Step 6, which would now read, "Determine the proportional contribution of the 1st, 2nd, and 3rd ranked prey for a diet that includes only the 1st, 2nd, and 3rd ranked prey." This and all the following steps would be computed just as before but now for a diet including the 3rd ranked prey — that is, for a diet including the 1st, 2nd, and 3rd ranked prey instead of just 1st and 2nd ranked prey. Steps 5–12 would be repeated again and again, adding successively lower ranking prey to the diet, until one encounters a prey whose handling return rate is too low to warrant inclusion in the diet.

ADVANCED TOPIC: ENERGETIC COSTS OF SEARCH AND HANDLING

In the spirit of keeping things simple, I have intentionally ignored the caloric costs of searching and handling. While these costs are potentially important, I have my reservations and have included this section mainly for completeness (see below "Do Energetic Search and Handling Costs

Matter Enough to Be Included in the Diet Breadth Model?"). For most students, especially those who think they've had enough trouble figuring out the basic diet breadth model, a quick reading of this section will suffice.

There can be no doubt that search and handling entail expenditures of energy that might affect resource ranking and diet breadth. While both search and handling costs are calculated in kcal, generally as kcal per unit of time, there are key differences in how we treat them. Handling costs apply to individual prey types; may differ by prey type (e.g., tracking, killing, and butchering a deer may be more physically taxing than clubbing and butchering a rabbit); and are always subtracted at the very start, before resources are ranked. Search cost, on the other hand, comes into play only when determining the foraging return rate (kcal/search+handling) for specific diet breadths and its cost per unit of time does not vary with diet breadth.

Incorporating Energetic Handling Cost

It is logical, of course, that kcal handling cost should be subtracted before resources are ranked. A resource that would otherwise be high ranking may well turn out to be low ranking once its handling costs are subtracted. (There's lots of gold left in the world that is simply too costly to mine, for example). It is easy to incorporate handling costs into resource rankings up front as part of Step 1. Simply subtract them to obtain net kcal values (prey kcal – prey kcal handling cost = net kcal) and calculate handling return rate in terms of net kcal. Step 1 would now change to read, "Rank prey by handling return rate (net kcal/handling time)." All remaining steps in calculating diet breadth would be computed using these net kcal values.

To illustrate, suppose all resources in the example we've been developing entail an energetic cost of 3 kcal/min of handling time. Resource ranking would now be in terms of net kcal values (kcal – kcal handling cost = net kcal), as shown in Table 1.13.

In this instance adding energetic handling cost produces rankings that are identical to those originally obtained. This is because we assumed that kcal expended per unit of handling time were the same for all three prey types. Since our original ranking was by kcal per unit of handling time, subtracting handling costs at the same rate for all prey types produces the same ranking while increasing the differences between prey types, making higher ranking prey relatively more attractive. Thus, without handling cost, the handling return rate for deer is 222% greater than for rabbit and 267% greater than for mice. When handling cost is set at 3 kcal/min for all prey types as in Table 1.13, the handling return rate for deer is 253% greater than for rabbit and 319% greater than for mice. Increasing handling costs to 5 kcal/min of handling time would make the handling return rate for deer 283% greater than for rabbit and 379%

Table 1.13. Characteristics of Prey Ranked by Net Kcal

	Deer	Rabbit	Mice
Kcal per item	100 kcal	75 kcal	25 kcal
Handling time per item	3 min	5 min	2 min
Kcal handling cost	–9 kcal	–15 kcal	–6 kcal
Net kcal per item	91 kcal	60 kcal	19 kcal
Net kcal/handling time	30.33 kcal/min	12.00 kcal/min	9.50 kcal/min
Rank by net kcal:	1st	2nd	3rd
Kcal/handling time	33.33 kcal/min	15.00 kcal/min	12.50 kcal/min
Rank by kcal:	1st	2nd	3rd

greater than for mice. In general, then, if they are roughly the same (per unit time) for all prey types, handling costs make high-ranking prey more attractive and in this way discourage widening of diet breadth. Quite predictably search costs have just the opposite effect.

Incorporating Energetic Search Cost

As noted earlier, the energetic costs of search are only computed when determining foraging return rates — that is, for specific diet breadths. This makes sense; there's no point calculating search costs for low-ranking prey types, which will never be searched for separately (i.e., they will always be searched for in combination with all higher ranking prey). For the same reason, while search cost per unit of time may vary from one habitat to the next (search may be more physically taxing in a closed jungle than an open savannah), it does not vary with changing diet breadth in the same habitat; that is, adding or deleting lower ranking prey does not change the cost of searching per unit of time cost. In our example, if while searching for a deer or rabbit one encounters a mouse, it is simply ignored. If diet breadth later expands to include mice, we are still searching for deer and rabbit (along with mice) — nothing that would affect cost per unit of search time changes, only search time itself. That said, the calculations needed to incorporate the caloric costs of search are simple. Suppose searching entails a cost of 3 kcal/min search. This would modify the foraging return rate originally calculated for the deer-only diet (Table 1.4), as shown in Table 1.14. In this case the previously obtained handling cost for deer (3 kcal/min handling) has already been subtracted, giving net kcal per item, from which search cost is next subtracted to give final kcal per item. Dividing this by foraging time produces a foraging rate of return that incorporates both handling costs (3 kcal/min handling) and search costs (3 kcal/min search).

Table 1.14. Foraging Return Rate for a Deer-Only Diet When Search and Handling Costs Are Deducted

	Deer-only diet
Net kcal per item	91.00 kcal
Search time per item	6.00 min
Handling time per item	3.00 min
= Foraging time per item	= 9.00 min
Search cost per item	−18 kcal
Final kcal per item	73.00 kcal
Final kcal/foraging time:	8.11 kcal/min

Step 3 would thus read, "Subtract kcal search cost per item from net kcal per item and calculate foraging return rate (final kcal/search+handling time) for the 1st ranked prey." Similarly, Step 11 would read, "Subtract kcal search cost per item from net kcal per item and calculate the foraging return rate (final kcal/search+handling time) for a diet that includes just the 1st and 2nd ranked prey."

As we would expect, the energetic costs of search decrease the attraction of the higher ranking prey because search time (thus kcal expended searching) always increases as diet breadth narrows. Search time (thus energetic search cost per item) is highest when diet breadth is at its narrowest, consisting of just the highest ranked prey. In this sense search cost and handling costs work against each other. Search cost favors widening of diet breadth; handling costs favor its narrowing.

Do Energetic Search and Handling Costs Matter Enough to Be Included in the Diet Breadth Model?

How much search and handling costs matter in the real world is a matter of conjecture. That search and handling take energy is clear; that this profoundly affects diet breadth in ways we can easily model quantitatively is not. At issue here is so-called Murphy's Law: "If anything can go wrong, it will." To include energetic search cost requires that one estimate kcal expended per unit of search time; the same goes for handling. Whether including these costs increases our ability to model a real-world situation depends on how good these estimates are—how confident we are that they match real-world conditions. Bad estimates are worse than no estimates at all. Every estimate we make entails a risk that we might estimate incorrectly—and you know what Murphy says. The problem is doubled here: if you're going to include one of these costs (say, handling cost), you have to include the other (search cost), since—for reasons discussed above—the two pull in opposite directions, search cost favoring wider diet breadth and handling cost favoring narrower diet breadth. Adding one but not the other guarantees bias. Risks also have a funny way of compounding themselves. Caloric expenditure during exercise varies directly with human body size, for example. So including energetic search and handling costs in our diet breadth model requires that we estimate not only the base rate of caloric expenditure, but also the size of the human expending it. Another estimate, another risk (Murphy again).

I know, I know: you're objecting that the diet breadth model requires that we estimate search time, handling time, and prey kcal. If we estimate those, why shouldn't we just plunge in all the way and estimate search and handling costs? The point is well taken but a bit wide of the mark. A variety of pretty good data stands behind our estimates of handling time, search time, and prey kcal. More to the point, the diet breadth model requires those estimates—without them there's no model. Sure, things can go wrong (as Murphy warns), but a diet breadth model limited to just those variables permits important insights while minimizing the number of things that can go wrong. Adding energetic search and handling costs into the mix substantially increases the number of things that can go wrong while producing only marginal gains in understanding.

With regard to formal modeling, then, call me a "Murphimizer": I favor minimizing possible error in the diet breadth model by omitting energetic handling and search cost. This does not mean we cannot employ insights about search and handling costs in making predictions. If something increases caloric expenditures during search (e.g., rainforest vs. savannah), for example, we can predict that diet breadth will widen. Likewise, if something increases calories expended while handling prey (e.g., need to work in subfreezing temperatures), diet breadth will narrow. There's enough in this model alone for a whole array of predictions with testable implications.

So if you skipped ahead to read this before slashing your way through the discussion of steps needed to incorporate energetic search costs and handling costs into the diet breadth model, and you're convinced by my argument, you may want to only briefly scan those parts— just be sure you know why you're convinced. If you're unconvinced, obsessive-compulsive, or want to know how to incorporate energetic search and handling costs simply because you find it interesting or think it might come in handy in cocktail party conversation, then pull out your pencil and paper, go back to the beginning of this section, and work through it. If you read this part last, having already worked through this section's more complicated parts, no decision is necessary. You're done!

FURTHER READING

Bettinger, R. L., and M. A. Baumhoff. (1982). The Numic Spread: Great Basin Cultures in Competition. *American Antiquity* 47:485–503.

The earliest application of the diet breadth and patch choice models to a real-world archaeological problem.

Charnov, E. L. (1976). Optimal Foraging: Attack Strategy of a Mantid. *American Naturalist* 110:141–151.
   An extraordinarily clear mathematical treatment of the logic of diet breadth.

Hawkes, K., K. Hill, and J. F. O'Connell. (1982). Why Hunters Gather: Optimal Foraging and the Ache of Eastern Paraguay. *American Ethnologist* 9:379–398.
   An exemplary and very early application of the diet breadth model to an ethnographic problem. Required reading for anyone interested in applying optimal foraging to hunter-gatherers.

MacArthur, R. H., and E. R. Pianka. (1966). On Optimal Use of a Patchy Environment. *American Naturalist* 100:603–609.
   Generally accepted as the earliest description of the diet breadth model and the closely related model of patch choice.

EXERCISES FOR CHAPTER 1

1.1. Rank the items in Table 1.15 from highest to lowest according to the diet breadth model.

Table 1.15. Data for Problem 1.1

	Pig	Frog	Elephant	Chicken	Dog
Kcal per item	250 kcal	10 kcal	5000 kcal	20 kcal	75 kcal
Search time per item	25 min	5 min	300 min	12 min	20 min
Handling time per item	20 min	3 min	600 min	30 min	25 min
Kcal/handling time	12.50	3.33	8.33	.67	3.00
Rank:					

1.2. Rank the items in Table 1.16 from highest to lowest according to the diet breadth model.

1.3. Determine the encounter rate (items/min) for each item from their search times as given in Table 1.17.

1.4. Again with reference to Table 1.17:

1.4A. What is the per item encounter rate and search time when diet includes just the 1st and 2nd ranked prey?

Table 1.16. Data for Problem 1.2

	Pronghorn	Mountain sheep	Jackrabbit	Marmot	Woodrat
Kcal per item	1000 kcal	2000 kcal	90 kcal	100 kcal	50 kcal
Search time per item	200 min	500 min	25 min	30 min	15 min
Handling time per item	90 min	120 min	10 min	10 min	8 min
Kcal/handling time	11.11	16.66	9	10	6.25
Rank:	2	1	4	3	5

1.4B. What is the per item encounter rate and search time when diet includes all three prey types (i.e., diet breadth = 1st&2nd&3rd ranked)?

1.5. Still again with reference to Table 1.17:

1.5A. What is the proportional contribution of the 1st and 2nd ranked prey when only those two are in the diet?

  →. fraxiur they contribute a encounter rate

1.5B. What is the proportional contribution of the 1st, 2nd, and 3rd ranked prey when all three are in the diet?

1.6. Using the data in Table 1.18:

1.6A. Determine the individual encounter rate for each item.

1.6B. Calculate search time and encounter rate per item for each possible diet breadth (i.e., diet breadth = 1st, 1st&2nd, 1st&2nd&3rd, 1st&2nd&3rd&4th, 1st&2nd&3rd&4th&5th).

1.7. Use the individual encounter rates obtained in Exercise 1.6A to calculate proportional contribution of each kind of item for each possible diet breadth.

1.8. In the chapter example, the handling return rate for the 3rd ranked prey did not warrant including it in the diet, implying this would produce a foraging return rate less than that for a diet including only deer&rabbit

Table 1.17. Data for Problems 1.3–1.5

Rank	1st	2nd	3rd
Search time per item	5 min	10 min	20 min
Encounter rate (items/min):			

Table 1.18. Data for Problems 1.6 and 1.7

Rank	1st	2nd	3rd	4th	5th
Search time per item Encounter rate (items/min):	10 min	1 min	5 min	4 min	2 min

(13.54 kcal/min). Using those data (given again in Table 1.19), calculate the foraging return rate when the 3rd ranked prey is included in the diet — that is, the foraging return rate for a diet that includes the 1st, 2nd, and 3rd ranked prey.

1.9. Kristen Hawkes, Kim Hill, and James O'Connell (1982; see "Further Reading") report that for Ache hunters the collared peccary (javelina, *Pecari tajacu*) is the 1st ranked species and red brocket deer (*Mazama americana*) is the 2nd ranked. The weights, kcal yield, and handling time for both species are shown in Table 1.20.

1.9A. To verify the ranking reported by Hawkes, Hill, and O'Connell (1982), find kcal/handling hr for collared peccary and red brocket deer.

1.9B. Hawkes, Hill, and O'Connell (1982) do not tell us the search time for either species, but we know that search time for the 1st ranked collared peccary must be high enough to justify taking the 2nd ranked red brocket deer upon encounter. How long must it take to locate a collared peccary to justify taking the 2nd ranked red brocket deer upon encounter (i.e., the point at which the handling return rate of the 2nd ranked red brocket is exactly the same as the foraging return rate for the 1st ranked collared peccary)? Assume that kcal expended in search and handling are small enough to be ignored.

ANSWERS TO CHAPTER 1 EXERCISES

1.1. Ranked from highest to lowest: Pig, Elephant, Frog, Dog, Chicken.

Table 1.19. Data for Problem 1.8

	Deer	Rabbit	Mice	Deer& rabbit&mice
Kcal per item	100 kcal	75 kcal	25 kcal	
Search time per item	6 min	2 min	1 min	
Handling time per item	3 min	5 min	2 min	
Kcal/foraging time:				

Table 1.20. Data for Problem 1.9

	Collared peccary	Red brocket deer
Kcal yield	39,000 kcal	24,570 kcal
Handling time	.60 hr	.90 hr
Kcal/handling hr:		

1.2. Ranked from highest to lowest: Mountain sheep, Pronghorn, Marmot, Jackrabbit, Woodrat.

1.3. Encounter rate (items/min): 1st = .20, 2nd =.10, 3rd =.05.

1.4A. Diet breadth = 1st&2nd: encounter rate = .30 items/min, search time = 3.33 min.

1.4B. Diet breadth = 1st&2nd&3rd: encounter rate = .35 items/min, search time = 2.86 min.

1.5A. Diet breadth = 1st&2nd: contribution of 1st = .67, contribution of 2nd = .33.

1.5B. Diet breadth = 1st&2nd&3rd: contribution of 1st = .57, contribution of 2nd = .29, contribution of 3rd = .14.

1.6A. Encounter rate (items/min) 1st = .10, 2nd = 1.00, 3rd = .20, 4th = .25, 5th = .50.

1.6B. Diet breadth = 1st: items/min = .10, search time = 10.00 min. Diet breadth = 1st&2nd: items/min = 1.10, search time = .91 min. Diet breadth = 1st&2nd&3rd: items/min = 1.30, search time = .77 min. Diet breadth = 1st&2nd&3rd &4th: items/min = 1.55, search time = .65 min. Diet breadth = 1st&2nd&3rd&4th&5th: items/min = 2.05, search time = .49 min.

1.7. Diet breadth = 1st: 1st = 1.00. Diet breadth = 1st&2nd: 1st = .09, 2nd = .91. Diet breadth = 1st&2nd&3rd: 1st = .08, 2nd = .77, 3rd = .15. Diet breadth = 1st&2nd&3rd &4th: 1st = .06, 2nd = .65, 3rd = .13, 4th = .16. Diet breadth = 1st&2nd&3rd&4th&5th: 1st = .05, 2nd = .49, 3rd = .10, 4th = .12, 5th = .24.

1.8. Kcal / foraging time = 13.19 kcal/min. Kcal/item = 47.50, the sum of kcal of each item weighted by its proportional contribution. Search time/item = .60 min, determined as inverse of sum of encounter rate for each item. Handling time/item = 3 min, the sum of handling time for each item weighted by its proportional contribution.

1.9A. Kcal/handling hr for collared peccary = 65,000; for red brocket deer = 27,300.

1.9B. Search time for collared peccary required to add red brocket deer to the diet is .83 hr, solved as follows:

kcal/(handling+search) for 1st	= kcal/handling for 2nd
kcal/foraging for collared peccary (1st)	= kcal/handling for red brocket deer (2nd)
$39{,}000 / (.60 + x)$	$= 27{,}300$
$39{,}000$	$= 27{,}300(.60 + x)$
$39{,}000$	$= 16380 + 27{,}300x$
$39{,}000 - 16380$	$= 27{,}300x$
$22{,}620$	$= 27{,}300x$
$22{,}620 / 27{,}300$	$= x$
$.83$	$= x$
$.83$ hr	= required search time

CHAPTER 2

OPTIMAL FORAGING WITH CONSTRAINTS: LINEAR PROGRAMMING

ALASKA, northeast of Anchorage. An Ahtna hunter is camped at the forks of a major river. One fork leads to a well-known upstream riffle where sockeye salmon (*Oncorhynchus nerka*) can be taken in relatively large numbers. The other fork passes through a small valley where word has it that beaver (*Castor canadensis*) are currently abundant. On this extended trip, the hunter needs to obtain both meat to feed his family and pack dogs and furs that can be traded for needed supplies (ammunition, traps, etc.). Salmon are certainly a cheaper source of meat than beaver but only beaver can supply the needed furs. The question, then, is how the hunter should spend the time he has before he must return downstream to his waiting family. His need for furs guarantees that some of his time will be spent trapping beaver. Still, should he make all his trips up the beaver fork for furs and meat or split his time, spending some of it catching salmon (the cheaper source of meat)? *Linear programming* is designed to address such situations.

INTRODUCTION

Linear programming is a non-contingency form of optimal analysis. In contingency models (e.g., diet breadth), the goal is to maximize momentary rates of return, which is why I call them "models of the moment." Circumstances of the moment define a contingency that presents a choice. In the case of the diet breadth model, the contingency is an encounter with a prey item presenting two (and only two) choices—take the prey item or pass it by and continue searching for higher ranked prey. The contingency contains all the information needed to make a rational choice: we know the expected return of the encountered prey and the expected return of passing it by and searching for higher ranked prey. To maximize expected rate of return, one simply chooses the better of the two alternatives. By contrast, linear programming deals with overarching goals rather than individual contingencies, and in that sense its solutions are strategic.

The heart of a linear programming model is a recipe of constraints or requirements. These are expressed with reference to important properties (e.g., kcal, vitamins, fat, procurement time) — commonly termed currencies — defining either upper limits that cannot be exceeded (maximum constraints) or lower limits that must be equaled or exceeded (minimum constraints). Thus the statement "I want a house with at least 2 bathrooms and no more than 3 fireplaces" defines the currency "bathroom" as a minimum constraint ($\geq$ 2 bathrooms) and the currency "fireplace" as a maximum constraint ($\leq$ 3 fireplaces). The same currency may be subject to different constraints. Thus I may have a "children's needs" constraint that requires a house with at least 2 bathrooms ($\geq$ 2 bathrooms) and also a "utility bill shock" constraint that demands a house with no more than 3 bathrooms ($\leq$ 3 bathrooms). Constraints are matched against existing resources (say, houses on the market) to determine which fit the bill, at which point additional currencies (e.g., price, age of house, neighborhood, etc.) may be used to make the best possible choice.

This points up a fundamental difference between contingency and linear programming models. Contingency models always have a solution. When presented two rates of return, one will be greater than or equal to the other; every diet breadth problem has an optimal rate of return. Linear programming problems may have no solution; the requirement that my house have no more than 3 fireplaces cannot be satisfied if every house on the market has more. The constraints themselves may be individually reasonable yet mutually incompatible: I cannot have a house that has more than 2 bathrooms (for all my children) and at the same time less than 2 bathrooms (to save water).

A more subtle difference between contingency and linear programming models hinges on the difference between benefits and costs on the one hand, and constraints on the other. In contingency models costs (e.g., time) and benefits (e.g., kcal) are distinct and there is just one of each. In linear programming both benefits (good stuff) and costs (bad stuff) are treated as constraints and there can be many of each. Situations with multiple benefits or costs require linear programming. I always use the "Ice Cream Cone Problem" to illustrate why this is so.

THE ICE CREAM CONE PROBLEM

Everyone knows that an ice cream cone has two parts, at a minimum 1 scoop of ice cream and 1 edible cone to hold it. Contingency models will handle the ice cream cone problem only if the ice cream and the cone always occur together as complete ice cream cones. If cost is at issue, it is easy to decide between an ice cream cone priced at $1 and an exactly identical ice cream cone priced at $2. The contingency scenario fails, however, if we want the cheapest possible ice cream cone but our local grocery store only sells ice cream and cones separately. Then we are presented no easy choice.

Suppose a package of 10 cones costs $1 and a 1-gallon carton of ice cream costs $5. The contingency solution—that we maximize rate of return—is meaningless here because cones and ice cream represent different currencies (utilities), both of them essential to making a complete ice cream cone. While a package of 10 cones priced at $1 is better than a package of 10 identical cones priced at $2, it is meaningless to ask whether a package of 10 cones priced at $1 is better than a 1-gallon carton of ice cream priced at $5. Solving this problem requires that we specify exactly what we want: 1 scoop of ice cream and 1 cone.

Linear programming makes it possible to cast this strategic goal with reference to available resources to determine the best possible solution to the problem. To see the difference, note that by contingency logic, $10 for a 5-gallon carton of ice cream beats $5 for a 1-gallon carton of the same ice cream. By linear programming logic, the opposite is true, at least if we only want 1 ice cream cone. Then $5 for 1 gallon beats $10 for 5 gallons. It makes no sense to pay $10 for 5 gallons of ice cream when we can pay $5 for 1 gallon, which is more than enough ice cream for 1 cone. Your local gas station *cum* convenience mart makes big bucks precisely for this reason.

AN EXAMPLE

As one might expect, given their added assumptions linear programming solutions are computationally more involved than most contingency model solutions, but the essential nature of one common approach is easily illustrated graphically for problems that involve only two potential resources. You can do this kind of modeling to a very close approximation using only graph paper. In this very simple method, the two resources are represented by the X- and Y-axes of a graph and constraints as lines running from the Y-axis to the X-axis.

Let's start with a simple problem to illustrate how such a model works. Let's assume we have two kinds of resources (quarters and $1 bills) that have a number of properties that might be useful or that might be liabilities. The most useful aspect of both, of course, is that they contain "exchange value"; that is, we can use them to get something else we want. On the other hand, they also have their liabilities. Value is a plus because we can use it to get things we want, and also a minus if there is some chance it can be taken from us. Similarly, quarters and $1 bills weigh something and are cumbersome to carry around in large amounts. But weight can also be useful in some circumstances.

We can illustrate how a linear programming model works by using these two currencies (weight and value) in connection with a simple problem. Let's say we want to go to a movie, and that since we're traveling through a rather sketchy part of town, we don't want to carry too much money (which might be stolen) or too much weight (which might hinder us from running from a possible threat). At the same time, we want to carry our money in a sock so we can use it to defend ourselves (I'm not suggesting you do this—it's an example!). To be more specific, assume the cost of entrance to the movie is $25 (it's a great movie!) and your sock needs to hold at least 8 grams (this won't stop anything larger than a cockroach, if that—but again it's an example). Further, assume that quarters weigh .50 grams and $1 bills weigh .25 grams (quarters weigh more and the ratio is obviously quite different—but play along with me here). The question is what combination of $1 bills and quarters will (a) allow us admission to the movie (at least $25) and (b) carry enough weight (at least 8 grams).

This is easily solved graphically by linear programming. We start, however, by tabulating the currencies and constraints as shown in Table 2.1, which will help us think more clearly.

Table 2.1. Values for the Quarter-$1 Bill Problem

	Value ($)	Weight (g)
Quarter (each)	.25	.50
$1 bill (each)	1.00	.25
Minimum required	25.00	8
Minimum in quarters	100	16
Minimum in $1 bills	25	32

To start we make a graph with quarters as the X-axis and $1 bills as the Y-axis (it could be the other way around, it doesn't matter, but we're doing it this way here). Now think of movie entrance as a minimal value constraint — we have to have at least $25 of value to get into the movie. Obviously both quarters and $1 bills contain value but in differing degree. If we carry only quarters, we'll need at least 100. If we carry only $1 bills, we'll need at least 25. This constraint can be graphed as a line connecting 100 on the X-axis (quarters) to 25 on the Y-axis ($1 bills), as in Figure 2.1.

This line defines an infinite number of quarter-$1 bill combinations, moving from all quarters to all $1 bills, that always add up to $25 in value. (Try to ignore that quarters and $1 bills only come in whole units of 1 so not all combinations are really possible in this special case; in most cases the resource can be infinitely divided—for example, acorn meal.) This line defines the constraint for value in our problem. We can get into the movie only with combinations of quarters-$1 bills that are on or above this line. Note that if the stipulation had been that we had to carry *more than* $25,

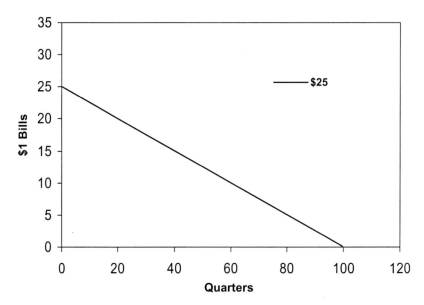

Figure 2.1. Value constraint in the quarter-$1 bill problem.

the constraint line would be the same, in this case plotting the margin of the constraint, which would not include quarter-$1 bill combinations totaling exactly $25 (i.e., on the line itself). Similarly, if we had to carry *exactly* $25, only combinations on the line itself would satisfy the constraint. In short, while constraints are always plotted as lines that represent limiting values, the nature of those limits can vary.

Now think of weight as another minimum constraint: we need to carry at least 8 grams in our sock to feel confident that we can defend ourselves. We can draw this constraint as a second line running from 16 quarters (at .50 grams each) to 32 $1 bills (at .25 grams each), as shown in Figure 2.2. Again, we have a line defining an infinite number of quarter-$1 bill combinations that always add up to 8 grams. We will feel confident only when carrying combinations of quarters and $1 bills that are on or above this line.

At this point we have all the information we need to solve our problem (Figure 2.3). First, we have defined a region of *feasible solutions*. The feasible region is minimally defined as the area including all non-negative values for X and Y (i.e., the resources they represent cannot take on negative values). Within these limits the feasible region for this problem is the shaded area that lies on or above the angled line formed by the intersection of our value and weight constraint lines. Any combination of quarters and $1 bills in this area will get the job done. At the same time, ours is a problem of minimization. We want to minimize both weight and value while meeting our constraints: we want enough weight, but just

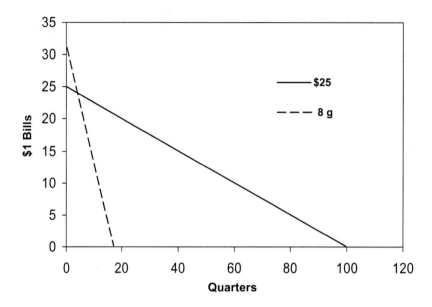

Figure 2.2. Value and weight constraints in the quarter-$1 bill problem.

enough—no more; and we want enough value, but just enough—no more. It follows that the combination of quarters-$1 bills that will (a) get us into the movie and (b) provide sufficient weight, while (c) keeping value to a minimum and (d) keeping weight to a minimum, will be on (not above) the joint value-weight constraint boundary or adjacent axes. In the graphical approach taken here, if this problem has a solution (this one does, but some don't), it will lie at one of the corners defined by this feasible region boundary—a corner being defined as a place where a constraint line intersects another constraint line or an axis boundary. The corner solutions are shown in Figure 2.3.

So let's examine the corners of the constraint boundary, starting with the one labeled A (the 8-gram constraint intersecting Y-axis), which is 32 $1 bills. As summarized in Table 2.2, A gets us into the movie (> $25) and provides sufficient weight (= 8 grams) but makes us carry $32, $7 more than we need. Next consider the corner marked C ($25 constraint intersecting X-axis), which is 100 quarters. Again, this gets us into the movie (= $25) and provides sufficient weight (> 8 grams) but makes us carry 50 grams, 42 grams more than we need. Finally, look at the corner marked B (intersection of the value and weight constraints), which is 4 quarters and 24 $1 bills (you can find this using graph paper at home). This gives us exactly enough money to get into the movie (= $25) and exactly enough weight to feel safe (= 8 grams), with no excess of either. We carry less value than with solution A and less weight than with solution C. We have

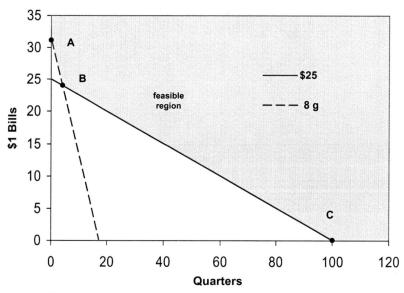

Figure 2.3. Feasible region and corner solutions to the quarter-$1 bill problem.

generated an optimal solution for going to a movie in a shady part of town. The two other examples given below apply this same kind of thinking to problems more appropriate to understanding hunter-gatherers.

Table 2.2. Solutions A, B, and C for the Quarter-$1 Bill Problem

		Value ($)	Weight (g)	
	Quarter (each)	.25	.50	
	$1 bill (each)	1.00	.25	
	Minimum required	25.00	8	
A	32 $1 bills	32.00	8	Too much value
C	100 quarters	25.00	50	Too much weight
B	4 quarters*	1.00	2	
	24 $1 bills*	24.00	6	
	Total	25.00	8	Just right

* While these values can be very closely approximated using graph paper, the exact values are easily determined using the method described in "Determining Values for Constraint Intersections."

A MAXIMIZING PROBLEM

The moviegoer example above depicts a minimizing problem. The object is to produce a specified quantity of one or more things in the cheapest possible way. Maximizing problems take the opposite tack, to produce the greatest possible quantity of something within specified production constraints. Here is an example.

Great Basin women commonly must forage and attend to household duties in the same day. This causes the goals of foraging to be different for them than for foragers whose only task is to optimize the rate at which they acquire and prepare food. The nature of the problem can be illustrated with reference to the activity of pinyon procurement.

Pinenuts, the seeds of the pinyon pine (*Pinus monophylla*), mature in late summer but remain tightly enclosed in sticky green cones until late fall, when the cones open and disperse their nuts. The nuts can be extracted in early fall from green cones through laborious processing, but we are concerned here with the activities surrounding the collection and processing of the nuts that occurs in late fall, when the cones have shed their nuts — which can be collected from the ground or easily shaken from brown cones on the ground or still attached to limbs. This is termed "brown-cone" procurement, the hypothetical return rates, gathering times, and processing times for which are summarized in Table 2.3.

Table 2.3. Values for the Brown-Cone Pinyon Procurement Problem

	Gathering time (hr)	Processing time (hr)	Total handling (hr)	Volume (l)	Kcal
Unhulled pinenuts (1 l)	2	0	2	1	500
Hulled pinenuts (1 l)	3	1	4	1	750
Maxiumum allowed			8	3	
Maximum in unhulled pinenuts (l)			4	3	
Maximum in hulled pinenuts (l)			2	3	

For women engaged in brown-cone procurement, there are three choices.

- They can gather as many nuts as possible (at 2 hr/l; see Table 2.3 above) and transport them unprocessed (unhulled) back to camp; since hulls are 33% of total nut volume (again, a hypothetical value), this means a good deal of useless material is transported. Further, while a woman can gather 4 liters of unhulled pinenuts in the allotted 8 hours of grove time, she can only bring home 3 liters. So choosing this option means she can only carry what she can collect in 6 hours (= 3 liters), wasting 2 hours of precious grove time.

- They can gather and hull all the nuts in the field. This results in the transport of only useful bulk (the nuts themselves) but entails more time in the field because the gatherer has to collect more nuts (more gathering time) and then process them (reducing volume by 33%) to generate the same 1 liter of volume. Specifically, to obtain 1 liter of hulled pinenuts, gatherers must collect for 3 hours to obtain 1.50 liters of unhulled nuts and then process them for 1 hour to remove and discard the .50 liters of hulls. However, choosing this option means they can collect and completely hull only 2 liters of nuts (= 6 hours collecting and 2 hours hulling), which means they go home with baskets that are only two-thirds full — wasting potential load capacity.

- They can gather nuts and process as many of them in the field as time permits. This might result in an optimal mix in which the amount of useless bulk transported is minimized and the payoff per unit of time spent in the field is maximized.

Our forager is thus operating under a number of constraints: most importantly she wants to *maximize* the calories she transports back to camp, subject to the two constraints: (a) a load constraint, because she can carry only 3 liters in her conical carrying basket; and (b) a time constraint, because she must return to camp before nightfall (her children and husband depend on her) and can only spend 8 hours in the pinyon grove.

To solve this problem, we plot the two kinds of resources involved — unhulled nuts and hulled nuts — as the X- (unhulled pinenuts) and Y- (hulled pinenuts) axes of a graph, as shown in Figure 2.4. Next we plot two constraint lines corresponding to the constraints of time and volume that must be satisfied. Each constraint line represents combinations of the two resources that will satisfy the constraint in question. For example, for the volume constraint (3 liters), it is clear that 3 liters of hulled pinenuts will satisfy the 3-liter constraint, as will 3 liters of unhulled pinenuts. Similarly, any 3-liter combination of hulled and unhulled pinenuts (say, 2 liters of hulled and 1 liter of unhulled) will also satisfy the 3-liter constraint. This can be plotted as a straight line connecting 3 liters X (unhulled pinenuts) and 3 liters Y (hulled pinenuts) on our graph. In Figure 2.4 it is the solid line labeled "3 l."

We follow the same logic to establish the 8-hour time constraint line. In this case 1 liter of unhulled nuts takes 2 hours to collect, therefore 4 liters in 8 hours, so 4 liters of unhulled nuts constitutes one point on the 8-hour constraint line. Similarly, to collect and hull 1 liter of (hulled) nuts takes 4 hours, therefore 2 liters in 8 hours, so 2 liters of hulled nuts constitutes a

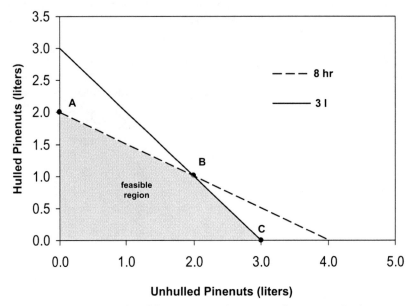

Figure 2.4. Constraints, feasible region, and corner solutions to the brown-cone pinyon procurement problem.

second point on the 8-hour line. Further, a straight line drawn between these two points on their respective axes—that is, between 4 liters on the unhulled nut, or X-axis, and 2 liters on the hulled nut, or Y-axis—denotes various combinations of hulled and unhulled nuts that will satisfy the 8-hour constraint. This is the broken line labeled "8 hr" in Figure 2.4.

Look at Figure 2.4 with these lines drawn: the two constraints define a region of feasible solutions, the corners of which are A, B, and C and the origin of the graph in the lower left corner. What we want to do is choose a point in this region that maximizes (remember this is a maximization problem) caloric yield. It is clear, to begin, that this point cannot be the origin of the graph (= no hulled or unhulled nuts); that is, it is not a feasible choice for our collector to collect nothing. It should be intuitively clear that since the more the better (again, this is a maximization problem), the boundary defined by points A, B, and C ought to be the place where we look for our maximal result. Further, it turns out that if the problem has a solution (and this one does), one of the points A, B, and C will be in that solution. This generalizes to all linear programming problems, which have the characteristic that if there is a solution, it will include one of the non-zero corners of the feasible region (here A, B, or C).

This being the case, all we have to do is calculate the energetic (kcal) value of the points A, B, and C, and select the one that yields the highest kcal return. As shown in Table 2.4, in this case we have:

Table 2.4. Solutions A, B, and C for the Brown-Cone Pinyon Procurement Problem

		Gathering time (hr)	Processing time (hr)	Total handling (hr)	Volume (l)	Kcal
	Unhulled pinenuts (1 l)	2	0	2	1	500
	Hulled pinenuts (1 l)	3	1	4	1	750
	Maximum allowed			8	3	
A	Hulled pinenuts (2 l)	6	2	8	2	1500
C	Unhulled pinenuts (3 l)	6	0	6	3	1500
B	Unhulled pinenuts (2 l)*	4	0	4	2	1000
	Hulled pinenuts (1 l)*	3	1	4	1	750
	Total	7	1	8	3	1750

* While these values can be very closely approximated using graph paper, the exact values are easily determined using the method described in "Determining Values for Constraint Intersections."

Clearly B yields the highest returns in kcal. Thus a female operating under a 3-liter, 8-hour constraint should spend 7 hours collecting nuts (= 3.50 liters) and 1 hour processing nuts (discarding .50 liters of hulls), from which she will gain 1750 kcal, which is higher than the value obtained for collecting and processing 2 liters of hulled nuts (1500 kcal) or collecting 3 liters of nuts (1500 kcal).

Let's pursue this a little further. Suppose we assume that the time constraint drops from 8 to 6 hours. This merely shifts the dotted line down to the left, parallel to its original slope. With this constraint there are only two choices: 3 liters of unhulled nuts (= 1500 kcal) or 1.50 liters of hulled nuts (= 1125 kcal). In this case the woman should collect but not process nuts. This illustrates two points—first that constraints are costly (reducing time by two hours reduces kcal returns by 250 kcal); and second that given the nature of pinenuts, the amount of processing should decrease as time constraints increase.

ANOTHER MINIMIZING PROBLEM

We have already worked through a minimizing problem in the moviegoer example above. Here is a more realistic example involving diet, a subject to which linear programming is often applied.

Table 2.5. Values for the Meat and Potatoes Diet Problem

	Calories	Protein (g)	Time (hr)
Potatoes (1 l)	100.00	10.00	1.50
Meat (1 l)	50.00	15.00	2.00
Minimum required	200.00	37.00	
Minimum in potatoes (l)	2.00	3.70	
Minimum in meat (l)	4.00	2.47	

In this problem we have two differently priced foods, meat and potatoes, each of which contains both protein and calories—nutrients we require. To be specific, let's say that we must expend 1.5 hours of labor (which is its price in this context) to obtain a liter of potatoes, which yields 100 kcal and 10 grams of protein (Table 2.5). By contrast, to obtain a liter of meat requires 2 hours of labor, which will yield 50 kcal and 15 grams of protein. Further, let's say that we want our diet to consist of at least 200 kcal and 37 grams of protein. We can graph these constraints in the same way that we graphed our earlier maximization problem, except of course that the axes and constraint lines take on different values and slopes.

In this case let's graph potatoes as the X-axis and meat as the Y-axis, as shown in Figure 2.5.

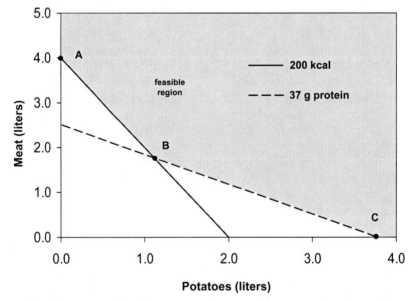

Figure 2.5. Constraints, feasible region, and corner solutions to the meat and potatoes diet problem.

The two constraint lines (one for kcal and one for protein) connect combinations of meat and potatoes that will produce the required quantities of 200 kcal and 37 grams of protein. Thus 4 liters of meat = 200 kcal and 2 liters of potatoes = 200 kcal, and the solid line connecting these two points indicates combinations of meat and potatoes that will also yield 200 kcal. For instance, the combination of 2 liters of meat (= 100 kcal) and 1 liter of potatoes (= 100 kcal) will yield 200 kcal (it's on the line, check it yourself!). Similarly, either 2.47 liters of meat or 3.70 liters of potatoes will yield 37 grams of protein, and the dotted line connecting these two points indicates combinations of meat and potatoes that together will yield 37 grams of protein.

As in the maximization problem above, the points labeled A, B, and C in Figure 2.5 define an area of feasible solutions. In this case, however, the feasible region is above—rather than below—the boundary, for only points on or above the boundary will yield the specified quantities of kcal and protein. Since our task is merely to meet these constraints in the cheapest possible (in this case least time-costly) fashion, it follows that if the problem has a solution (and this one does), it will be right on the boundary, which indicates the smallest quantities of either meat or potatoes or meat-potatoes combination needed to meet our requirements (the cheapest solution). Furthermore, owing to the nature of our graph, one of the corner points A, B, and C will be included in that solution.

Simple: all we have to do is calculate the time costs for the three corner points to find the least time-costly solution to our minimization problem. Here (as shown in Table 2.6) we find that:

Table 2.6. Solutions A, B, and C for the Meat and Potatoes Diet Problem

		Calories	Protein (g)	Time (hr)
	Potatoes (1 1)	100.00	10.00	1.50
	Meat (1 1)	50.00	15.00	2.00
	Minimum required	200.00	37.00	
A	4.00 l of meat	200.00	60.00	8.00
C	3.70 l of potatoes	370.00	37.00	5.55
B	1.15 l of potatoes*	115.00	11.50	1.73
	1.70 l of meat*	85.00	25.50	3.40
	Total	200.00	37.00	5.13

* While these values can be very closely approximated using graph paper, the exact values are easily determined using the method described in "Determining Values for Constraint Intersections."

So the combination B of meat (1.70 liters) and potatoes (1.15 liters) is the cheapest way to obtain 200 kcal and 37 grams of protein. Easy, isn't it? Note also that while the optimal solution in all the examples given here is the one where the two constraint lines intersect, that is not always so. You always have to check all the corners. (Too often I have made this mistake and missed the optimal solution!)

DO CONSTRAINT LINES ALWAYS INTERSECT?

In all our examples, the constraint lines intersect, meaning that resources are differentially suited to constraints: each resource does a better job with one of the two constraints. Let me explain. In all our examples, there are two resources and two constraints, and in each case it takes less of the X-axis resource to satisfy one of the constraints (say, constraint A) than the other constraint (say, constraint B). Conversely, it takes less of the Y-axis resource to satisfy constraint B than constraint A; that way the two constraint lines will cross. Confused? Well, it's hard to convey in words but easy to see when graphed. In the Meat and Potatoes example above, it takes fewer potatoes (2 liters) to satisfy the 200-kcal calorie constraint than it does to satisfy the 37 grams of protein constraint (3.70 liters of potatoes). Conversely, it takes less meat (2.47 liters) to satisfy the 37-gram protein constraint than it does to satisfy the 200-kcal calorie constraint (4 liters of meat). Potatoes do a better job with calories than protein, and meat does a better job with protein than calories. See?

But what if for both resources it takes less to satisfy constraint A than constraint B—that is, if both do a better job with constraint A than constraint B? Then the two lines will not intersect: the A constraint line will lie completely below the B constraint line, both running down to the right (but see "Do Constraint Lines Always Run Down-to-the-Right?" below) but never touching. The feasible region will then depend on the nature of the constraints. If the lower line (here A) represents a minimum constraint and the upper line (here B) represents a maximum constraint, the feasible region will lie between the two—that is, above A and below B. You must check the four corners of this feasible region for an optimal solution: the X-axis and Y-axis intercepts of the lower line and the X-axis and Y-axis intercepts of the upper line. If both lines represent minimum constraints, the feasible region will lie above the upper line B. That is, the solution must lie above A and above B, the area below A and between A and B not satisfying the second condition (above B). This feasible region has only two corners that need checking for an optimal solution: the X-axis and Y-axis intercepts of the upper line. By like reasoning, if both lines represent maximum constraints, the feasible region will lie below the lower line A; that is, the solution must lie below A and below B, the area above B and between A and B not satisfying the first condition (below A). Again, this feasible region has only two corners that need checking for an optimal solution: the X-axis and Y-axis intercepts of the lower line. Finally, if the lower line A represents a maximum constraint and the upper line B represents a minimum constraint, the problem has no solution. There is no feasible region since no point can at the same time be below A and above B.

DO CONSTRAINT LINES ALWAYS RUN DOWN-TO-THE-RIGHT?

The simple answer is "No." Most of the ones we're interested in do, but even some of them do not. When they don't, it means one of the two resources does not contribute to the constraint in question. In the Ice Cream Cone example, for instance, no amount of ice cream can satisfy the cone constraint, nor can any amount of cones satisfy the ice cream constraint. In such cases the line (or boundary) for the single-resource constraint will run perpendicular to the axis representing the resource that contributes to the constraint and parallel to the axis of the resource that does not contribute to the constraint. If we make ice cream the X-axis and cones the Y-axis, the "at least 1 scoop" constraint will be a perpendicular line anchored at $X = 1$ and the "at least 1 cone" constraint will be a horizontal line anchored at $Y = 1$, making the feasible region all possible combinations that contain at least 1 scoop and at least 1 cone—thus the area on or above the horizontal line and on or to the right of the perpendicular line. This feasible region has only one corner: the intersection of the two where $X = 1$, $Y = 1$.

For sake of completeness, I should mention that resource constraints can run up-to-the-right, in which case one resource is working against its alternative, subtracting from its contribution. Suppose, in our Ice Cream Cone Problem, cones possessed some kind of "anti-ice cream" property, every cone somehow magically causing 1 scoop of ice cream to disappear. Then to build our 1 complete cone, we would need 1 cone and 2 scoops of ice cream. There are many real-world interactions of this sort (e.g., nutrients that work against each other), but in the interest of clarity I'm going to ignore their possibility in the remaining discussion. That said, up-to-the-right constraints are really not all that difficult to puzzle out and interested students should have no trouble working through them on their own.

DETERMINING VALUES FOR CONSTRAINT INTERSECTIONS

As we have seen above ("Do Constraint Lines Always Intersect?"), constraint lines do not always intersect. When they do and their intersection is part of the boundary of the feasible solution for the problem, that intersection defines a corner that must be checked to determine whether it represents an optimal solution to the problem. This can be done to a close approximation using graph paper, but the exact values for the intersection of any two constraint lines in a two-resource problem are readily determined using the equations for each constraint. In the special case where a constraint can only be satisfied by one resource, the other neither adding nor subtracting (see above "Do Constraint Lines Always Run Down-to-the-Right?"), this equation is trivially simple. It is simply the amount of the resource needed to satisfy the constraint in units of the axis representing that resource. As noted above, if we make ice cream the X-axis, the "at least 1 scoop" constraint will be a perpendicular line anchored at $X = 1$, that limiting value providing the equation for that constraint $X = 1$. Similarly, if cones are the Y-axis, the "at least 1 cone" constraint will be a horizontal line anchored at $Y = 1$, that limiting value providing the equation for that constraint $Y = 1$.

Where both resources can be used to satisfy a constraint, the constraint line will run down to the right (again, see above "Do Constraint Lines Always Run Down-to-the-Right?") and its equation will take the form you may recall from high school algebra:

$Y \qquad = aX + b \qquad\qquad$ where

$X \qquad$ is any given X-axis value

$Y \qquad$ is the corresponding Y-axis value

$a \qquad$ is the slope of the constraint line

$b \qquad$ is the Y-intercept of the constraint line (i.e., the value of Y when $X = 0$)

Since Y is a function of X, and X can be any value we want, we need only know the values for b and a, which are easily found. The first thing to do is decide which resource is represented by the X-axis and which by the Y-axis: it doesn't matter which is which as long as they are always the same for all constraints. Now the Y-axis intercept of the constraint line b is obvious; it's just the value of Y that will satisfy the constraint — the value we used to draw the constraint line from the Y-axis to the X-axis. So if it takes 30 units of the Y resource to satisfy a constraint, $b = 30$ for that constraint. Simple, isn't it? To obtain the slope of the constraint line a, we also have to know the X-axis intercept of the constraint line, which is simply the amount of the X resource that will satisfy the constraint. Suppose it takes 15 units of the X resource to satisfy the constraint. Then the slope of the constraint line a is simply:

$$a = -(Y\text{-axis intercept} / X\text{-axis intercept})$$

$$= -(30 / 15)$$

$$= -2$$

Thus the equation for the constraint we've just described is:

$$Y = aX + b$$

$$= -2X + 30$$

To see how this works, note the Y value we obtain when $X = 15$, meaning the constraint is completely satisfied by the X resource. Clearly, when $X = 15$ then $Y = 0$ ($Y = -2 \times 15 + 30 = 0$), which is as it should be — the constraint being completely satisfied by the X resource. By like reasoning, when the constraint is completely satisfied by the Y resource, then X will obviously have to be $X = 0$. And when $X = 0$, then $Y = -2X + 30 = 30$, as it should be. This explains why the slope of the constraint line is negative. The constraint is a fixed value that must be satisfied by the sum of the X resource and Y resource. Since their sum is constant, if one increases, the other must decrease, so the sign of the slope is always negative, its value indicating the rate at which substitution occurs. The slope $a = -2$ means that 2 units of Y substitute for 1 unit of X. Conversely a slope of $a = -1/2$ means that 1 unit of Y substitutes for 2 units of X. As a reminder, the exception is when one of the two resources does not contribute to the constraint in question (see above "Do Constraint Lines Always Run Down-to-the-Right?"). Since there is no substitution in these cases, the relationship $Y = aX + b$ does not apply. Instead, as we have seen, the constraint is expressed simply as the value of the resource needed to satisfy it.

The "Meat and Potatoes Diet Problem" (see Table 2.5) poses the more common situation where each resource contributes to each constraint. The calorie constraint (200 kcal) can be satisfied by 2 liters of potatoes (X resource) or 4 liters of meat (Y-axis), so we use the relationship $Y = aX + b$ and get:

$$a = -4 / 2 = -2$$

$$b = 4$$

$$Y = -2X + 4$$

The protein constraint (37 g) can be satisfied by 3.70 liters of potatoes (X resource) or 2.47 liters of meat (Y resource), so:

a = -2.47 / 3.70 = -.67

b = 2.47

Y = -.67X + 2.47

The whole point of this rather long-winded exposition is to find the intersection of two constraints, each described by an equation. This means finding the unique values for X and Y that will simultaneously satisfy both equations, which is where the two lines intersect. There are three possibilities here.

Two Single-Resource Constraints

If both constraints are of the kind that can only be satisfied by one of the two resources (see "Do Constraint Lines Always Run Down-to-the-Right?"), you already have the answer; the equations tell you everything you need to know. For example, if the equation for one constraint is $X = 34$ and for the other constraint $Y = 24$, that's your answer: they intersect where $X = 34$ and $Y = 24$. Of course if the equation for one constraint is $X = 34$ and for the other constraint $X = 24$, or for one constraint $Y = 34$ and for the other $Y = 24$, there will be no intersection.

One Single-Resource Constraint and One Two-Resource Constraint

If one constraint can only be satisfied by one of the two resources, the other potentially satisfied by either, simply substitute the limiting value for the single-resource constraint into the equation for the two-resource constraint. Suppose the limiting value for the single-resource constraint is $X = 10$ and the equation for the two-resource constraint is $Y = -2X + 30$. Simply substitute the value for the single-resource constraint into the equation for the two-resource constraint:

Y = -2X + 30

       = -2(10) + 30

       = -20 + 30

       = 10

Their intersection is thus $X = 10$, $Y = 10$.

Suppose, however, the values were $Y = -2X + 30$ and $X = 25$. Then:

Y = -2X + 30

$$= -2(25) + 30$$

$$= -50 + 30$$

$$= -20$$

The negative value here means the two constraint lines do not intersect within the feasible region, which—as noted at the outset—excludes negative values for any resource. You'll find it easier all along the way if you crudely graph constraints, which will generally tell you whether they are likely to intersect and thus whether it is worth attempting to solve for their intersection.

Two Two-Resource Constraints

The last kind of intersection is also the one in which we are most interested—that of two constraints, each of which can be satisfied with either of our two resources and which do in fact intersect (again, you may want to review "Do Constraint Lines Always Intersect?"). Here both constraint lines will slant down to the right, the equations for each taking the form $Y = aX + b$, giving us $Y = a_1X + b_1$ for the first constraint and $Y = a_2X + b_2$ for the second. Solving for their intersection is easy. All we have to do is let the first equation be equal to the second equation and solve for X. That is, let $Y = a_1X + b_1$ be equal to $Y = a_2X + b_2$. Easy. Just drop the Ys and it looks something like this:

$$a_1X + b_1 = a_2X + b_2$$

This can be juggled—as shown in Appendix 2—to give $X = (b_2 - b_1)$ / $(a_1 - a_2)$, which is the X-axis value of the intersection of the two constraints X_{intsct}. The Y-value of the intersection is easily obtained by substituting this X-value (i.e., of X_{intsct}) into either constraint equation. Translated into plain English, to obtain X_{intsct} for the intersection of two constraints:

X_{intsct} $= (b_2 - b_1) / (a_1 - a_2)$ where

b_1 is the Y-intercept of the first constraint

b_2 is the Y-intercept of the second constraint

a_1 is the slope of the first constraint

a_2 is the slope of the second constraint

So for the meat and potatoes problem, letting calories be the first constraint and protein the second, we get:

$$\text{kcal } Y = -2X + 4, a_1 = -2, b_1 = 4$$

$$\text{protein } Y = -.67X + 2.47, a_2 = -.67, b_2 = 2.47$$

$$X_{intsct} = (b_2 - b_1) / (a_1 - a_2)$$

$$= (2.47 - 4.00) / (-2.00 - [-.67])$$

$$= (2.47 - 4.00) / (-2.00 + .67)$$

$$= -1.53 / -1.33$$

$$= 1.15$$

The value $X_{intsct} = 1.15$ represents the value of X (i.e., the quantity of potatoes, 1.15 liters) at the intersection of the two constraints. To obtain the corresponding value of Y (quantity of meat), simply substitute the value of X_{intsct} into either of the constraint equations. For the calorie equation, this gives:

$$Y_{intsct} = -2X_{intsct} + 4$$

$$= -2(1.15) + 4$$

$$= -2.30 + 4$$

$$= 1.70$$

And for the protein equation, we get the same result:

$$Y_{intsct} = -.67X_{intsct} + 2.47$$

$$= -.67(1.15) + 2.47$$

$$= -.77 + 2.47$$

$$= 1.70$$

So the intersection occurs where X (potatoes) = 1.15 and Y (meat) = 1.70.

To make sure these values are correct, we should see whether this combination of meat and potatoes produces the required constraints for calories (200 kcal) and protein (37 grams), given that potatoes generate 100 kcal/l and meat 50 kcal/l, and potatoes generate 10 grams protein/l and meat 15 grams protein/l. And as you can see below (Table 2.7), indeed they do. Whew — that was a lot of work!

Table 2.7. Intersection Solution for Meat and Potatoes Problem

		Potatoes		Meat		
	amount l	1.15		1.70		
Kcal constraint (≥ 200 kcal)	x kcal / l	100.00		50.00		
	= kcal	115.00	+	85.00	=	200.00
Protein constraint (≥ 37 g)	x g protein / l	10.00		15.00		
	= g protein	11.50	+	25.50	=	37.00

FURTHER READING

Belovsky, G. E. (1987). Hunter-Gatherer Foraging: A Linear Programming Approach. *Journal of Anthropological Archaeology* 6:29–76.

Belovsky describes himself as a population/community ecologist. This paper is among the most thorough and thoughtful applications of linear programming to ethnographic hunter-gatherers. It provides the basis for Exercises 2.5–2.11 below.

Keene, A. S. (1981). *Prehistoric Foraging in a Temperate Forest: A Linear Programming Model.* Academic Press, New York.

An early application of linear programming to a real-world archaeological example.

Reidhead, V. A. (1979). Linear Programming Models in Archaeology. *Annual Reviews in Anthropology* 8:543–578.

A thorough review of the logic and literature of linear programming as applied to archaeological problems.

EXERCISES FOR CHAPTER 2

2.1. A group of hunters is poised at a famous ambush location where the men expect to kill many buffalo, enough that they will require a fair amount of butchering tools. They think that about 250 microblades will get the job done — but so will 23 bifaces. What is the nature of the butchering constraint (maximum or minimum) and, letting microblades be the X-axis resource, what is its equation?

2.2. These hunters also figure that—what with scouting and working on the gear that will actually be used in the hunt—they have about half a day to devote to stone tool working, which will allow for the making of 300 microblades or 12 bifaces. What is the nature of the knapping time constraint and, again letting microblades be the X-axis resource, what is its equation?

2.3. Plot these lines on graph paper, and if they appear to intersect, compute their intersection.

2.4. What is the shape of the feasible region containing all the possible biface-microblade combinations that simultaneously satisfy both the hunters' butchering constraint and their knapping time constraint? How many corners does it have and what are their X, Y coordinates?

2.5. Gary Belovsky (1987; see "Further Reading") calculated that to satisfy their own caloric requirements and that of their immediate dependents (e.g., children), each !Kung adult had to have food amounting to at least 3042 kcal, which could be satisfied with either 997 grams of vegetable food or 1014 grams of meat.

2.5A. How many kcal does each gram of vegetable food produce?

2.5B. Each gram of meat? (I know this is pretty basic but we're starting slow here; it's going to get more complicated as we go on.)

2.6. Belovsky (1987) also calculated that, counting time contributed by dependent helpers, each !Kung has no more than 519 minutes per day to spend acquiring food. If all of that is given to obtaining and preparing plants, 1133 grams of (vegetable) food are obtained. If all of it is given to obtaining and processing game, 1184 grams of meat are obtained.

2.6A. How many minutes are required to generate each gram of vegetable food produce?

2.6B. Each gram of meat?

2.7. Calculate the rate at which kcal are obtained by !Kung:

2.7A. Engaged in plant procurement and processing.

2.7B. Engaged in game procurement and processing.

2.8. If we make vegetable food the X-axis, what is the equation for the !Kung kcal constraint? Graph this constraint.

2.9. Again making vegetable food the X-axis, what is the equation for the !Kung time constraint? Add this constraint to the previous graph—the one already showing the kcal constraint.

2.10. On the graph depicting the kcal and time constraints, identify and label the feasible region.

2.11. Belovsky (1987) calculated that counting dependent input, each adult !Kung *actually* obtains and prepares about 805 grams of vegetable food and 342 grams of meat for personal consumption or distribution to dependents.

2.11A. How many minutes per day is each adult !Kung (and helpers) devoting to plant and animal procurement?

2.11B. How many kcal per day is each adult !Kung (and dependents) consuming?

2.12. Plot actual adult !Kung vegetable and meat consumption on the graph on which you have previously entered the kcal and time constraints and identified the feasible region. If kcal and time are the most important constraints on !Kung hunting and gathering, what is limiting this activity?

ANSWERS TO CHAPTER 2 EXERCISES

2.1. As shown in Figure 2.6, it is a minimum constraint: the hunters must have *at least* 250 or 23 bifaces to butcher the expected kill. Its equation is:

$$Y = aX + b$$

$$= -(23 / 250)X + 23$$

$$= -.09X + 23$$

2.2. It is a maximum constraint (Figure 2.6): the hunters have only enough time to make 300 microblades or 12 bifaces. Its equation is:

$$Y = aX + b$$

$$= -(12 / 300)X + 12$$

$$= -.04X + 12$$

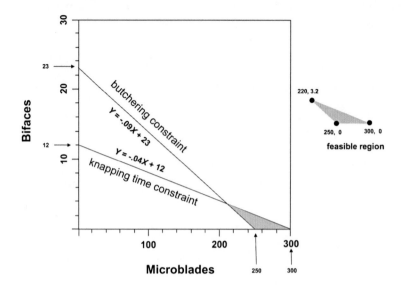

Figure 2.6. Graphic depiction of the biface-microblade problem.

2.3. They do appear to intersect (Figure 2.6). Their intersection is obtained by solving first for the intersection relative to the X-axis, and using that value X_{intsct} to obtain the intersection for the Y-axis from both constraint equations.

Solving first for the X-axis intersection X_{intsct}:

$$X_{intsct} = (b_2 - b_1) / (a_1 - a_2)$$

$$= (12 - 23) / (-.09 - [-.04])$$

$$= (-11) / (-.05)$$

$$= -11 / -.05$$

$$= 220 \text{ microblades}$$

Solving next for the Y-axis intersection Y_{intsct} for the butchering constraint:

$$Y_{intsct} = -.09X_{intsct} + 23$$

$$= -.09(220) + 23$$

$$= -19.80 + 23$$

$$= 3.20 \text{ bifaces}$$

Solving next for the Y-axis intersection Y_{intsct} for the knapping time constraint:

$$Y_{intsct} = -.04X_{intsct} + 12$$

$$= -.04(220) + 12$$

$$= -8.80 + 12$$

$$= 3.20 \text{ bifaces}$$

2.4. The feasible region is a triangle resting on the X-axis with its peak skewed to the left (Figure 2.6). It has three corners. Their X, Y coordinates are lower left, 250, 0; lower right, 300, 0; peak, 220, 3.20.

2.5A. 3042 kcal / 997 g vegetable = 3.05 kcal/g vegetable.

2.5B. 3042 kcal / 1014 g meat = 3.00 kcal/g meat.

2.6A. 519 min / 1133 g vegetable = .46 min/g vegetable.

2.6B. 519 min / 1184 g meat = .44 min/g meat.

2.7A. 3.05 kcal/g vegetable / .46 min/g vegetable = 6.63 kcal/min vegetable.

2.7B. 3.00 kcal/g meat / .44 min/g meat = 6.82 kcal/min meat.

2.8. See Figure 2.7:

$$Y = -aX + b$$

$$= -(1014 / 997)X + 1014$$

$$= -1.02X + 1014$$

2.9. See Figure 2.7:

$$Y = -aX + b$$

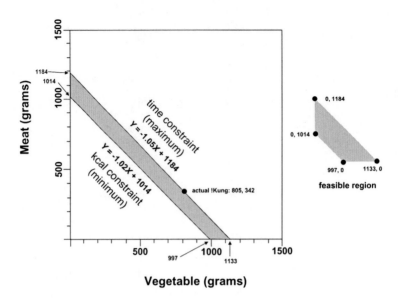

Figure 2.7. Graphic depiction of the !Kung diet problem.

$$= -(1184 / 1133)X + 1184$$

$$= -1.05X + 1184$$

2.10. See Figure 2.7. It is the area above the energy constraint line (minimum constraint) and below the time constraint line (maximum constraint) — that is, between them.

2.11A. 520.78 min/day = (805 g vegetable x .46 min/g vegetable) + (342 g meat x .44 min/g meat).

2.11B. 3481.25 kcal/day = (805 g vegetable x 3.05 kcal/g vegetable) + (342 g meat x 3.00 kcal/g meat).

2.12. Time. The !Kung are consuming more food than they actually require; they are above that minimal constraint. They are hunting and gathering as much as available time will allow. See Figure 2.7.

CHAPTER 3

FRONT- AND BACK-LOADED RESOURCES: CACHING

WESTERN UTAH, Trout Creek area, late July. A Gosiute woman and her elderly mother are camped with the rest of their family in a large valley flanked by a long, pinyon (*Pinus monophylla*) covered ridge, which the family has selected as its likely wintering spot. The pinyon trees on this particular ridge are loaded with immature and unripe cones that they expect to harvest in September, caching them in quantity as their major winter food source. While the pinyon crop looks large enough to last through a normal winter, there is always the possibility that spring will come later than usual or that heat spells, insect infestations, or gusty summer dust storms will prevent some of the cones from maturing, reducing the crop.

Accordingly, in addition to gathering and preparing seeds and roots for their daily needs, these two Gosiute women are accumulating extra seeds and roots for winter use. The wild crops from which they can choose differ in their characteristics. On the one hand, roots and seeds are equally easy to store once they are acquired, but some roots require heavy digging and are thus harder to accumulate in quantity than most seeds. On the other hand, roots are essentially ready to eat once they are harvested, while seeds almost always require extensive processing to make them palatable. The question is how the Gosiute women should divide their time between easy-to-acquire but hard-to-prepare seeds and hard-to-acquire but easy-to-prepare-roots. The *front-back loading model* is designed to address such cases.

INTRODUCTION

The front-back loading model is designed to address what we all know: nearly every problem has two solutions, one quick and dirty and the other not. The quick and dirty solution is cheap in the short run but costly in the long run. Its alternative is more costly in the short run but more efficient in the long run. The obvious question is "If the quick and dirty solution is likely to be costly in the long run, why would anyone choose it?" Laziness or inability to pay the higher cost of its alternative, perhaps—but more likely because there is some chance the "long-run" outcome is unlikely and we're willing to take that chance. Such choices are a matter of everyday life. Take car insurance. One can pay a very low annual premium in exchange for a very high deductible (the amount your insurance company deducts from the amount it estimates will be needed to repair accident damage) or a higher premium in exchange for a lower deductible. Other things being equal, individuals who select the low-premium option are more willing to bet they won't be involved in an accident than are individuals who opt for higher premiums.

Technology provides another example. Ever own one of those Swiss Army knives with a knife blade, scissors, flathead and Phillips head screwdrivers, and corkscrew? If so, you probably bought it not so much for any one of those potential functions but as a quick and dirty solution for all of them. Sure, the corkscrew will *probably* work as a last resort, but you won't see any wine steward—*sommelier* if you're a wine snob—with one; nor would you likely take it along on a picnic when your picnic basket included a bottle of wine, in which case you'd bring a "real" corkscrew. (If you want to know what the "dirty" in "quick and dirty" means, just try opening a bottle of wine with a Swiss Army knife corkscrew!) Paradoxically you carry the Swiss Army knife with the corkscrew precisely because you really *don't* expect to encounter a bottle of wine that needs opening, but like a good Boy Scout you want to be prepared just in case one should magically appear out of nowhere.

No less than ourselves, hunter-gatherers faced the same sort of quick and dirty versus costly and efficient options, not only in technology but in a host of other affairs that required assessing the probability of this or that eventuality. Storage and caching are one important example.

THE MODEL

Imagine the situation faced by mobile hunter-gatherers when they first began experimenting with caching. For these groups the goal of caching would be to obtain a surplus of resources for use on future occasions when the only resources available would be costly because they were scarce, time-consuming to procure and process, or both. With access to caches, these groups could ride out periods of resource shortfall and grow in size beyond the limits these shortfalls imposed. Nevertheless a gamble was involved since the extra effort expended in obtaining and processing excess resources for caching would be wasted in the event that the need for them did not subsequently arise.

Groups initially experimenting with caching must have been particularly sensitive to this risk. Resources would still have been fairly abundant relative to group size, and the mobility needed to take advantage of shifting resource concentrations might be compromised were these groups to remain too closely tethered to caches they might never use. Because of this, it's safe to assume that many of the caches made by groups first experimenting with this behavior went unused—either because cheaper resources continued to be readily available, or because the group moved too far away before they were needed. The resources that would be selected for caching under these conditions would not necessarily be those with the lowest per kcal handling times, handling time for a cached resource being the total amount of time expended in procuring it, processing it for caching (including construction of the cache), and later preparing it for consumption. It is convenient here to divide the handling time for stored resources into two components.

z Storage time: the time required to acquire and process a resource for storage.

c Culinary time: the time needed to prepare the stored resource for final consumption.

A distinction is then possible between "back-loaded" resources that are cheap to acquire and store but costly to prepare for consumption, and "front-loaded" resources that are costly to acquire and store but subsequently easy to prepare for consumption. The contrast is important because while resource caching requires acquisition and storage, it does not require preparation unless the cache is actually used. Because of this, a resource that is characterized by very high overall handling times (since it is excessively costly to prepare for consumption) may still be favored for caching if its storage time is very low, and if the probability the cache will be used is also low. Some resources are obviously front loaded; salmon come to mind— costly to catch and dry, easy to prepare. Others are more back loaded; pinenuts are a good example—nut-bearing cones are easy to collect and store but separating nut from cone and preparing them for consumption is costly. Ultimately, however, the front-back distinction is relative. Pinenuts are probably back loaded in comparison to grass seeds (which are much more costly to acquire) and at the same time front loaded in comparison to acorns (which are very easy to collect and store but very costly to process because they must be leached to remove tannic acid). For this reason the front-back loading model deals with pairs of resources that stand in specific relationship to each other: a back-loaded resource that has a lower storage time $z_1 < z_2$, where z_1 is storage time for the back-loaded resource and z_2 is storage time for the front-loaded resource; and a front-loaded resource that has a lower overall handling time $z_2 + c_2 < z_1 + c_1$, where c_1 is culinary time for the back-loaded resource and c_2 is culinary time for the front-loaded resource. Each resource thus offers a different kind of advantage as a candidate for caching.

The back-loaded resource has an initial advantage because it is cheap to cache in bulk. It will be the best choice if the cache ends up not being used. The front-loaded resource has a deferred advantage because it is cheaper overall. It will be the best choice if the cache ends up being used. So deciding between them will hinge on the probability q that the cache will be used, which makes it possible to determine the expected cost of either choice.

For example, the expected cost of the back-loaded resource is its cost if the cache is used $(z_1 + c_1)$ times the probability the cache is used (q) plus its cost if the cache is not used (z_1) times the probability the cache will not be used $(1 - q)$, or $q(z_1 + c_1) + (1 - q)z_1$. By like reasoning, the expected cost of the front-loaded resource is $q(z_2 + c_2) + (1 - q)z_2$. Critical here is the point above which q is large enough to favor the front-loaded resource, and below which it is small enough to favor the back-loaded resource. This is obtained by solving for q for the equation in which the expected returns of the front and back-loaded resources are exactly equal:

$$q(z_1 + c_1) + (1 - q)z_1 = q(z_2 + c_2) + (1 - q)z_2$$

As shown in Appendix 3, solving for q gives:

$$q = z_2 - z_1 / c_1 - c_2$$

This value of q defines what may be regarded as the *probability switching point* $q_{1 \leftrightarrow 2}$ between the back- and front-loaded resource:

$$q_{1 \leftrightarrow 2} = z_2 - z_1 / c_1 - c_2$$

Below this value the probability of cache use favors the back-loaded resource with the initial storage advantage, while above it the front-loaded resource with the deferred culinary advantage is favored, as graphically shown in Figure 3.1.

There is another way to interpret $q_{1 \leftrightarrow 2}$. Suppose we stipulate the cache is always used but that the *fraction* of it that is used varies. Under these conditions $q_{1 \leftrightarrow 2}$ is the *proportion of use switching point*. This makes perfect sense if you think about it for a minute in the logic of Abraham Lincoln, who observed, "You can fool some of the people all of the time, and all of the people some of the time." In our case you can use 100% of the cache 50% of the time or 50% of the cache 100% of the time—either way, only 50% of the cache ends up being used. In addition to being easy to compute, the equation $q_{1 \leftrightarrow 2} = z_2 - z_1 / c_1 - c_2$ is essentially foolproof. We don't even have to know ahead of time where a pair of resources stands in the prescribed front-back loaded

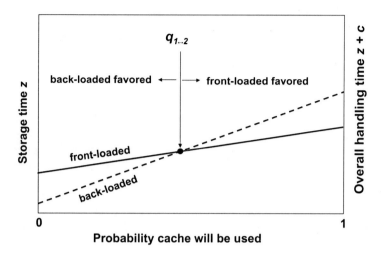

Figure 3.1. Front-back loaded problem graphically depicted. Axis on the left represents storage time, axis on the right overall handling time (storage time + culinary time). Back-loaded resource is initially cheaper (to store) but ends up being more costly (storage time + culinary time) if the cache is actually used. $q_{1\leftrightarrow2}$ is the probability of cache use at which both resources are equally costly. When actual probability is lower, the back-loaded resource is favored; when actual probability is higher, the front-loaded resource is favored. If the cache is always used but in variable amounts, $q_{1\leftrightarrow2}$ is the proportion of use at which both resources are equally costly.

relationship; we can figure that out from the results of the equation. When two resources stand in the classic front-back relationship, one with an initially lower advantage in storage time and the other with a deferred advantage in overall handling time, the switching point equation will kick out a value greater than 0 and less than 1. This is so no matter how we label our two resources: we can make pinenuts resource 1 and acorns resource 2, or acorns resource 1 and pinenuts resource 2. More formally, if $z_1 < z_2$ and $z_2 + c_2 < z_1 + c_1$ (or $z_2 < z_1$ and $z_1 + c_1 < z_2 + c_2$, which amounts to the same thing with the labels shuffled), then $0 < z_2 - z_1 \ / \ c_1 - c_2 < 1$.

Rule 1

When $0 < q_{1\leftrightarrow2} < 1$, resource 1 and resource 2 stand in a front-back loaded relationship that gives the resource with the lower storage time an initial advantage (making it the best choice when $q < q_{1\leftrightarrow2}$) and gives the resource with the lower overall handling time a deferred advantage (making it the best choice when $q > q_{1\leftrightarrow2}$). This is the kind of situation depicted in Figure 3.2A.

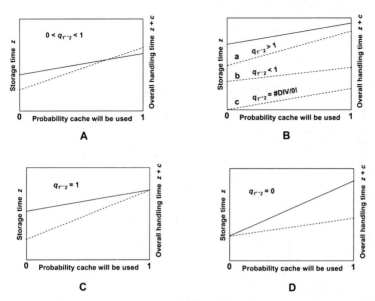

Figure 3.2. Different possible relationships between two resources. A depicts a classic pair of front-back loaded resources. B depicts different situations in all of which the resource represented by the solid line is inferior to the ones represented by the broken lines. C depicts a situation in which the resource represented by the solid line is inferior to the one represented by the broken line if there is any chance at all the cache will not be used (i.e., $q < 1$). D depicts a situation in which the resource represented by the solid line is inferior to the one represented by the broken line if there is any chance at all the cache will be used (i.e., $q > 1$).

However, what if $q_{1 \leftrightarrow 2}$ turns out to be greater than 1?

Rule 2

When $q_{1 \leftrightarrow 2} > 1$, the resource with the smaller storage time has the smaller overall handling time and is thus the best choice whether or not the cache is used. Since $q_{1 \leftrightarrow 2} = z_2 - z_1 / c_1 - c_2$, $q_{1 \leftrightarrow 2} > 1$ would obviously mean that $z_2 - z_1 > c_1 - c_2$. Translated into plain English, the difference between the storage times of the two resources $z_2 - z_1$ would be greater than their difference in culinary times $c_1 - c_2$. Not much of a problem, you say? Well, it would then follow that $z_1 + c_1 < z_2 + c_2$, meaning that the resource with the lower storage time also has the lower overall handling time, beating its alternative on both counts. This is the kind of situation depicted in Figure 3.2Ba, where the solid line and the dotted line labeled "a" will intersect to the right of the graph. As you can see from the total range of possible relationships depicted in Figure 3.2, $q_{1 \leftrightarrow 2}$ simply tells us where the two lines representing our two resources will intersect—in this case to the right of the graphed area. The take home message here is that the front-back relationship only applies if the deferred advantage of the front-loaded resource is greater than the initial advantage of the back-loaded resource (i.e., $c_1 - c_2 > z_2 - z_1$).

Okay, what if $q_{1 \leftrightarrow 2} = 1$? If you guessed this means the two lines intersect at 1, you're right.

Rule 3

When $q_{1 \leftrightarrow 2} = 1$, the resource with the lower storage time will be favored if $q < 1$. Since $q_{1 \leftrightarrow 2} = z_2 - z_1 / c_1 - c_2$, if $q_{1 \leftrightarrow 2} = 1$ then obviously $z_2 - z_1 = c_1 - c_2$ and thus $z_1 + c_1 = z_2 + c_2$. In plain words here the difference in the storage time is exactly the same as the difference in the culinary time; the overall handling times of the two resources are identical. However, since they will end up being equally costly only if the cache is used, the resource with the lower storage time—the one with the initial advantage—will end up being less costly anytime there is any chance the cache will not be used. This is the kind of situation depicted in Figure 3.2C.

But what if $q_{1 \leftrightarrow 2} = 0$? If you guessed this means the two lines intersect at 0, you're right again.

Rule 4

When $q_{1 \leftrightarrow 2} = 0$, the resource with the lower culinary time will be favored if $q > 0$. Since $q_{1 \leftrightarrow 2} = z_2 - z_1 / c_1 - c_2$, when $q_{1 \leftrightarrow 2} = 0$ then obviously $z_2 - z_1 = 0$, which means $z_1 = z_2$ (i.e., the storage times of the two resources are the same). This means the resource with the smaller culinary time will have the smallest overall handling time (obviously if $z_1 = z_2$ and $c_1 > c_2$, then $z_1 + c_1 > z_2 + c_2$). While the two resources start out being equally costly ($z_1 = z_2$), that equality only holds if there is no chance the cache will be used (i.e., $q = 0$). In any other instance, even if there is only the slightest chance the cache will be used, the resource with the smaller culinary time (and thus the smaller overall handling time) has the advantage. This is the kind of situation depicted in Figure 3.2D.

Yeah, yeah . . . but what if $q_{1 \leftrightarrow 2}$ is negative (i.e., $q_{1 \leftrightarrow 2} < 0$)?

Rule 5

When $q_{1 \leftrightarrow 2} < 0$ (negative), the resource with the smaller storage time is universally superior. Again, since $q_{1 \leftrightarrow 2} = z_2 - z_1 / c_1 - c_2$, that $q_{1 \leftrightarrow 2} < 0$ would obviously mean that either $z_2 - z_1 < 0$ (negative) or $c_1 - c_2 < 0$ (negative), but not both—in which case $q_{1 \leftrightarrow 2}$ is positive. Think about this for a minute and you will see that when $q_{1 \leftrightarrow 2}$ is negative, the resource with the smaller storage time has to be universally superior to the other. For example, when $z_2 - z_1 < 0$ (negative) and $c_1 - c_2 > 0$ (positive), then $z_2 < z_1$ and $c_2 < c_1$: resource 2 is universally superior; it has both the initial and deferred advantage. By exactly the same logic, when $z_2 - z_1 > 0$ (positive) and $c_1 - c_2 < 0$ (negative), then $z_1 < z_2$ and $c_1 < c_2$—meaning resource 1 is universally superior, having both the initial and deferred advantage. This is the kind of situation depicted in Figure 3.2Bb, where the solid line and the dotted line labeled "b" will intersect to the left of the graph.

Okay, what if computing $q_{1\leftrightarrow2}$ requires dividing by zero, something that is mathematically impossible? When this happens the spreadsheet program Excel® balks and simply returns a value of #DIV/0!, for example.

Rule 6

If computing $q_{1\leftrightarrow2}$ requires dividing by zero, the resource with the smaller storage time is universally superior. Again, since $q_{1\leftrightarrow2} = z_2 - z_1 / c_1 - c_2$, if computing $q_{1\leftrightarrow2}$ requires dividing by zero, then obviously $c_1 - c_2 = 0$; therefore $c_1 = c_2$, meaning the two resources have exactly the same culinary time. In that case the resource with the lower storage time will also have the lower overall handling time and thus will always be favored (i.e., if $z_1 < z_2$ and $c_1 = c_2$, then $z_1 + c_1 < z_2 + c_2$). This is the kind of situation depicted in Figure 3.2Bc, where the solid line and the dotted line "c" are exactly parallel and will never intersect! The obvious exception here is when $z_2 = z_1$ and $c_1 = c_2$, which means the two resources are exactly identical. (You don't need math to figure out that no math is needed in that case!) A summary of these rules is provided in Table 3.1.

Table 3.1. Relationship of Two Resources as Defined by $q_{1\leftrightarrow2}$

Rule	Value of $q_{1\leftrightarrow2}$	Relationship
1	$0 < q_{1\leftrightarrow2} < 1$	Two resources stand in classic front-back loaded relationship
2	$q_{1\leftrightarrow2} > 1$	Resource with smaller storage time universally superior
3	$q_{1\leftrightarrow2} = 1$	Resource with smaller storage time favored if $q < 1$
4	$q_{1\leftrightarrow2} = 0$	Resource with smaller culinary time favored if $q > 0$
5	$q_{1\leftrightarrow2} < 0$	Resource with smaller storage time universally superior
6	$q_{1\leftrightarrow2} = $ #DIV/0!	Resource with smaller storage time universally superior

The front-back model tells us that when hunter-gatherers first began caching, when residential itineraries were highly flexible and probability of cache use (i.e., q) was relatively small, back-loaded resources would likely have been chosen for caching to minimize storage time. This storage-time bias would remain, even when caching became common, provided there remained the possibility of switching to fresh resources whose overall handling times were lower than the preparation time of the cached resource.

We can generalize the caching/storage version of the front-back model to any situation where there are initial costs that must be paid and deferred costs that may not have to be paid. Here the probability switching point $q_{1 \leftrightarrow 2}$ is simply:

$$q_{1 \leftrightarrow 2} \quad = (i_2 - i_1) / (d_2 - d_1) \quad \text{where}$$

i_1 is initial cost for the back-loaded alternative

i_2 is initial cost for the front-loaded alternative

d_1 is deferred cost for the back-loaded resource

d_2 is deferred cost for the front-loaded resource

given $i_2 > i_1$ and $i_1 + d_1 > i_2 + d_2$.

FURTHER READING

Bettinger, R. L. (1999). From Traveler to Processor: Regional Trajectories of Hunter-Gatherer Sedentism in the Inyo-Mono Region, California. In *Settlement Pattern Studies in the Americas: Fifty Years Since Virú*, edited by B. R. Billman and G. M. Feinman, pp. 39–55. Smithsonian Institution Press, Washington, DC.

The original publication of the front-back loading model described here.

EXERCISES FOR CHAPTER 3

3.1. Given the values for storage and culinary times in Table 3.2, calculate the critical probability of cache use (or critical proportion of use) $q_{1 \leftrightarrow 2}$ for each pair of resources and the rule that applies to their relationship (e.g., Rule 1, classic front-back loaded relationship). If one resource is universally superior, so indicate.

3.2. Robert Bettinger, Ripan Malhi, and Helen McCarthy (1997; see "Further Reading," Chapter 5) report that it takes Western Mono women (California) 1.53 hours to gather and dry for storage a quantity of black oak (*Quercus kellogii*) acorns that, with another 26.74 hours of processing,

Table 3.2. Data for Problem 3.1

	Storage hr	Culinary hr
Apples	1	5
Oranges	2	3
Cherries	25	60
Tomatoes	51	15
Salmon	25	60
Clams	55	30
Peas	130	60
Beans	200	25
Potatoes	142	27
Asparagus	125	25
Ducks	142	25
Geoducks	125	25
Rice	1	5
Millet	1	3

will be a batch of meal worth 22,215 kcal. James O'Connell and Kristen Hawkes (1981, Alyawara Plant Use and Optimal Foraging Theory, in *Hunter-Gatherer Foraging Strategies: Ethnographic and Archaeological Analysis*, edited by B. Winterhalder and E. A. Smith, pp. 99–125, University of Chicago Press, Chicago) report that it takes the Alyawara of central Australia 2.84 hours to gather, and another 1.14 hours to process into edible form, the caloric equivalent of that in *Ipomea* root. The Alyawara do not normally store *Ipomea* root for any length of time, but suppose they did and this required no additional storage time beyond gathering. Suppose further that Alyawara women also had access to black oak and could gather and process it as efficiently as Western Mono women.

3.2A. Which of the two would be the front-loaded resource and what would be the critical probability of cache use $q_{1 \leftrightarrow 2}$ required to justify caching it?

3.2B. How would the answer to 3.2A change if storing *Ipomea* root required 10 hours of drying?

ANSWERS TO CHAPTER 3 EXERCISES

3.1. Pair, $q_{1\leftrightarrow2}$, rule, explanation: Apples/oranges, .50, Rule 1, classic front-back relationship. Cherries/tomatoes, .58, Rule 1, classic front-back relationship. Salmon/clams, 1.00, Rule 3, resource with smaller storage time favored if $q < 1$. Peas/beans, 2.00, Rule 2, resource with the smaller storage time universally superior. Potatoes/asparagus, –8.50, Rule 5, resource with the smaller storage time universally superior. Ducks, geoducks, #DIV/0!, Rule 6, resource with smaller storage time universally superior. Rice/millet, 0.00, Rule 4, resource with smaller culinary time favored if $q > 0$.

3.2A. Acorn is back loaded, *Ipomea* front loaded. The critical probability of cache use $q_{1\leftrightarrow2}$ is .05; above that *Ipomea* is favored.

3.2B. Acorn is still back loaded, *Ipomea* still front loaded. The critical probability of cache use $q_{1\leftrightarrow2}$ is now .44; above that *Ipomea* is favored.

CHAPTER 4

TECHNOLOGICAL INVESTMENT

CALIFORNIA, middle Klamath River, September. It is late in the salmon (*Oncorhynchus tshawytscha*) season and most Karok families have already filled their winter quota. Among those who have not is a ne'er-do-well whom nobody much likes. He's pretty good with his carefully crafted two-pronged toggling harpoon but lazy and too much given to gambling. As a case in point, on this morning he looks down on the Klamath without his valued harpoon, which he lost last night during a spirited bout of gambling. This unfortunate Karok is in a tough spot. On the one hand, he needs to lay in more salmon for the winter and the salmon run is quickly drawing to a close. But on the other hand, he lacks the proper tools and no one is going to lend him any: he's going to have to make his own from scratch. He sees two alternatives. One is to fashion another two-pronged toggling harpoon. This is undeniably the most effective tool for taking salmon but making and assembling its many separate parts will take a lot of time. The other is to settle for a simpler tool—a one-pronged toggling harpoon or a simple barbed spear—that will be less effective but take less time to make. Which should he chose? The *technological investment model* is designed to address just this sort of problem.

INTRODUCTION

This simple model of technological investment (sometimes referred to as the *tech investment model*) is designed to understand how primitive technology evolves, and in particular when it will pay for hunter-gatherers to invest more of their time making tools and facilities that improve success in resource procurement. The technological investment model helps us understand this simple bottom line: the more time hunter-gatherers spend getting resources, the more it pays for them to invest in procurement technology. We have previously encountered exactly the same logic in the front-back loading model, where we compared a "quick and dirty"

59

solution to a more costly — but more efficient — alternative. We applied the front-back loading model to the special case of resource caching but noted that it might just as easily apply to problems of technology (e.g., Swiss Army knife corkscrew vs. wine steward's corkscrew).

As will become clear shortly, while it differs in details, the technological investment model is similar in form to the front-back loading model and equally easy to understand and apply. If you can do that one, you can do this one! If you *can't* do that one, maybe this one will help straighten you out. The chief difference is that front-back loading problems, much like linear programming problems, are posed with reference to a predetermined goal or constraint (e.g., opening *exactly* three bottles of wine or caching *exactly* 10,000 kcal of food). Holding this goal constant, the front-back loading model examines costs to find a critical probability (the probability that the goal will be met) above which an initially costlier, and below which an initially cheaper, alternative is favored. By contrast, technological investment problems are not built around a specific, predetermined goal. Instead, as with contingency models (e.g., diet breadth), the goal of technological investment is merely to maximize payoff relative to cost in the special case where payoff varies with cost — when there is the possibility of obtaining higher payoffs if one is willing to pay higher costs.

THE MODEL

Let's start with two key variables and their symbols.

m_i Manufacturing time: the time spent making a particular kind of procurement technology i, expressed here in hours.

r_i Procurement rate: the rate at which a resource is obtained using technology i, expressed here in kcal per hour.

For instance, in Figure 4.1 technology A is characterized by its manufacturing time m_A; by the rate at which kcal are procured using it r_A; and by their relationship r_A / m_A, the rate at which manufacturing time increases rate of procurement (i.e., investing m_A produces a return rate of r_A). Technological evolution and change can then be thought of as a competition between technologies characterized by different combinations of r_i, m_i, and r_i / m_i, some inherently superior to others. It is simplest to think about this for cases in which there are two alternative technologies. For either of the pair to be competitive in the presence of the other, it must satisfy one of two conditions.

Stop! A warning before we proceed. The following sections are a bit dense and can be confusing if you move too fast, so take your time and be

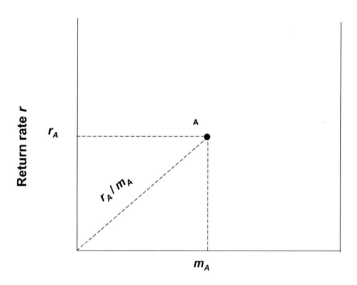

Manufacturing time _m_

Figure 4.1. Technology A is characterized by its manufacturing time m_A, by the rate at which kcal are procured using it r_A, and by the rate at which manufacturing time increases rate of procurement r_A/m_A.

sure you understand each part before proceeding. Refer to the illustrations and don't be afraid to back up and start over. Ready? Here, then, are the conditions needed to make one technology viable in the presence of another.

Condition 1. The more costly technology must produce a higher rate of return.

It would be foolish to invest time in making a tool that produced lower returns than a cheaper one. By definition, then, if manufacturing time of one technology is greater than that of its competitor, then its procurement rate must also be greater than that of its competitor. Formally:

$$\text{if } m_2 > m_1, \text{ then } r_2 > r_1$$

For instance, in Figure 4.2 any technology in the section marked "1" is superior to technology A; the technologies in section 1 are either cheaper with a higher rate of procurement, equally costly with a higher rate of procurement (right boundary of section 1), or equally productive but cheaper (lower boundary of section 1). Similarly, technology A is superior to any technology in the section marked "4," relative to which A is either cheaper with a higher rate of procurement, equally costly with a higher rate of procurement (left boundary of section 4), or equally productive but cheaper (upper boundary of section 4). In terms of technological

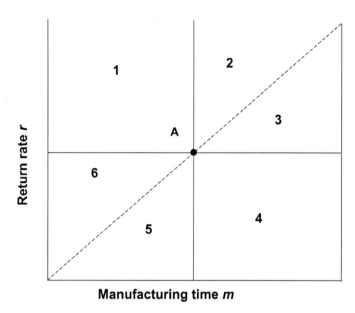

Figure 4.2. Technology A relative to other possible technologies. Sections defined as follows: section 1, $m_1 \le m_A$, $r_1 \ge r_A$; section 2, $m_2 > m_A$, $r_2 > r_A$, $r_2 / m_2 > r_A / m_A$; section 3, $m_3 > m_A$, $r_3 > r_A$, $r_3 / m_3 \le r_A / m_A$; section 4, $m_4 \ge m_A$, $r_4 \le r_A$; section 5, $m_5 < m_A$, $r_5 < r_A$, $r_5 / m_5 < r_A / m_A$; section 6, $m_6 < m_A$, $r_6 < r_A$, $r_6 / m_6 \ge r_A / m_A$.

evolution, the invention of technology A would immediately make all technologies in section 4 forever obsolete; technology A would be a "technological breakthrough." Similarly, the invention of any technology in section 1 would immediately make technology A obsolete.

Condition 2. The technology with the lower return must produce a rate of return per unit of manufacturing time at least equal to that of the technology with the higher return.

Lower returns can only be justified by lower costs: lower, more costly returns make no sense (see Condition 1). Condition 2 says that the low-return technology must not merely be cheaper; it must be cheap enough to make it at least equivalent to the higher return alternative in terms of rate of return per unit of manufacturing time. This will be true, for instance, if manufacturing time increases procurement efficiency at a diminishing rate—more manufacture time producing incrementally smaller gains in procurement than are obtained at lower levels of investment in manufacture. When that is so, the highest payoff per unit of manufacturing time (i.e., of technological investment) occurs with the "cheapest" (least time costly) technologies. To be competitive, then, a low-return technology must be cheap enough to generate a rate of return *per unit of technological investment* that is no worse than that of the more costly, higher return technology. If a cheaper technology instead generates a lower rate of return per unit of manufacturing time, that manufacturing time is better spent on the more costly technology, which generates both higher returns *and* larger increases in procurement per unit of technological investment. Formally:

if $r_1 < r_2$, then $r_1/m_1 \geq r_2/m_2$

In Figure 4.2 any technology in section 2 is superior to technology A, because A produces both a lower rate of return *and* a lower rate of return relative to manufacturing time. In turn, technology A is superior to any technology in section 5, relative to any of which technology A produces both a higher rate of return *and* a higher rate of return relative to manufacturing time. Here again the invention of technology A would be a technological breakthrough, immediately making all technologies within section 5 obsolete, just as the invention of any technology in section 2 would be a technological breakthrough rendering technology A obsolete.

In sum, Conditions 1 and 2 permit us to reason that for technology A to be competitive, its alternative cannot fall in sections 1, 2, 4, or 5. Knowing this might be useful. Finding the remains of technology A in an archaeological site, for example, would tell us that—other things being equal—the group responsible for those remains lacked technologies with the combinations of r_i, m_i, and r_i / m_i that define sections 1, 2, 4, or 5. It would not, however, preclude the possibility that they possessed technologies characterized by the combinations defining sections 3 and 6. This is because technology A is mutually competitive with any technology in sections 3 or 6, just as any technology in 3 is mutually competitive with any technology in 6. In all three combinations, the more costly technology provides a higher rate of return and the lower return technology provides at least an equivalent return per unit of manufacturing time, jointly satisfying Conditions 1 and 2. See for yourself in Table 4.1.

In most places, most of the time, the available array of technology will be like this—a combination of cheap technologies that produce returns that are low in absolute terms but high relative to manufacturing time, and costly technologies that produce returns that are high in absolute

Table 4.1. Relationships in Figure 4.2

A & 3	A & 6	3 & 6
$m_3 > m_A$	$m_A > m_6$	$m_3 > m_6$
$r_3 > r_A$	$r_A > r_6$	$r_3 > r_6$
$r_A / m_A \geq r_3 / m_3$	$r_6 / m_6 \geq r_A / m_A$	$r_6 / m_6 \geq r_3 / m_3$

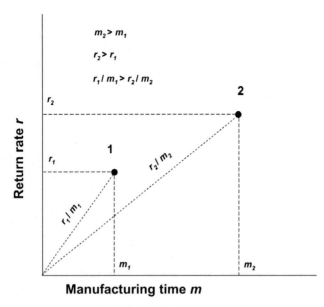

Figure 4.3. Two mutually competitive technologies, 1 and 2. Technology 2 is more costly but produces a higher rate of return. Technology 1 produces a lower rate of return but is so much cheaper to produce that it generates a higher rate of return relative to manufacturing cost.

terms but low relative to manufacturing time. The pair of technologies shown in Figure 4.3 illustrates the situation. These two technologies can coexist because each is viable under the right conditions.

Note that if we leave the matter right here, and consider return rate r only in relation to manufacturing time m, the costlier technology m_2 will make sense only in the special case $r_1 / m_1 = r_2/m_2$. If $r_1 / m_1 > r_2 / m_2$, the cheaper technology wins both ways: it's cheaper ($m_1 < m_2$) and provides more procurement bang for the manufacturing buck ($r_1 / m_1 > r_2 / m_2$). However, the more costly technology may still make sense if procurement returns are parsed not only in relation to manufacturing time, but to other time costs associated with procurement, the most obvious being procurement time itself.

s Procurement time: the total amount of time expended in procurement of a resource, again expressed in hours.

When procurement time s is included, the object becomes one of maximizing returns r_i relative to the sum of manufacturing time and procurement time—that is, of maximizing $r_i / (m_i + s)$ rather than r_i / m_i. This is important because even when $r_1 / m_1 > r_2 / m_2$, since $r_2 > r_1$, if s is large enough, then $r_2 / (m_2 + s) > r_1 / (m_1 + s)$. This is shown by the solid line in

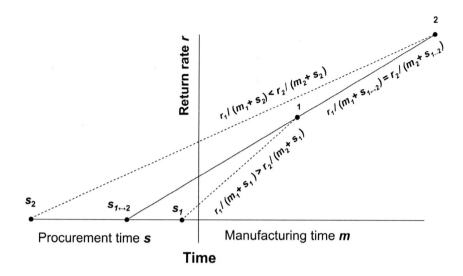

Figure 4.4. When procurement time is equal to $s_{1\leftrightarrow2}$, cheaper and more costly technologies produce exactly the same rate of return. When procurement time is greater (e.g., s_2), the costlier technology produces a higher rate of return. When it is less (e.g., s_1), the cheaper technology produces a higher rate of return.

Figure 4.4, where the return rate of the two are just equal at $s_{1\leftrightarrow2}$. When procurement time is greater than $s_{1\leftrightarrow2}$, the costlier technology produces a higher rate of return. When it is less than $s_{1\leftrightarrow2}$, the cheaper technology produces a higher rate of return.

It is easy to find out how large procurement time s has to be to justify the more costly technology by solving for s in the equation:

$$r_2 / (m_2 + s) = r_1 / (m_1 + s)$$

As shown in Appendix 4, solving for s gives:

$$s = (r_1 m_2 - r_2 m_1) / (r_2 - r_1)$$

We can define this particular value of s as $s_{1\leftrightarrow2}$, the *procurement time switching point* between technology 1 and technology 2. Above this switching point ($s > s_{1\leftrightarrow2}$), the more costly technology is favored, and below it ($s < s_{1\leftrightarrow2}$) the cheaper technology is favored. The formula to remember, then, is:

$$s_{1\leftrightarrow2} = (r_1 m_2 - r_2 m_1) / (r_2 - r_1)$$

For an example, suppose we have the two technologies depicted in Table 4.2.

Table 4.2. Example Data

	Technology 1	Technology 2
Manufacturing time (hr) m	$m_1 = 1$	$m_2 = 3$
Procurement rate (kcal/hr) r	$r_1 = 1$	$r_2 = 2$
r/m	$r_1/m_1 = 1.00$	$r_2/m_2 = .67$

Note that Conditions 1 and 2 above are satisfied. The more costly technology 2 produces higher returns (2 > 1). The lower return technology 1 produces at least equivalent returns per unit of manufacturing time (1.00 > .67).

By the formula for $s_{1 \leftrightarrow 2}$ above:

$$s_{1 \leftrightarrow 2} = (r_1 m_2 - r_2 m_1) / (r_2 - r_1)$$

$$= (1*3 - 2*1) / (2 - 1)$$

$$= (3 - 2) / 1$$

$$= 1$$

And we can see that at this critical procurement time switching point $s_{1 \leftrightarrow 2}$ = 1, the two technologies do indeed produce the same rate of return:

$$r_2 / (m_2 + s_{1 \leftrightarrow 2}) = r_1 / (m_1 + s_{1 \leftrightarrow 2})$$

$$2 / (3 + 1) = 1 / (1 + 1)$$

$$2 / 4 = 1 / 2$$

$$.50 = .50$$

To make sure we understand what's going on, let's try a problem with different values (Table 4.3).

Table 4.3. Example Data

	Technology 1	Technology 2
Manufacturing time (hr) m	$m_1 = 3$	$m_2 = 5$
Procurement rate (kcal/hr) r	$r_1 = 1$	$r_2 = 2$
r/m	$r_1/m_1 = .33$	$r_2/m_2 = .40$

So just plug the values into our equation for $s_{1\leftrightarrow2}$:

$$s_{1\leftrightarrow2} = (r_1m_2 - r_2m_1) / (r_2 - r_1)$$

$$= (1{*}5 - 2{*}3) / (2 - 1)$$

$$= (5 - 6) / 1$$

$$= -1 / 1$$

$$= -1$$

Wait a minute! I got −1. Is that what you got? Well, −1 can't be right: there's no such thing as negative procurement time! What went wrong? Well, actually the numbers are right. The problem here is that the technologies fail to meet the conditions needed to make them mutually competitive. Remember them? In this case the more costly technology 2 produces higher returns (2 > 1), fulfilling that condition. However, the lower return technology 1 does not produce at least equivalent returns per unit of manufacturing time (.33 < .40), so condition 2 is not fulfilled. These technologies are not mutually competitive. The more costly technology 2 beats the cheaper technology 1 regardless of procurement time. It produces higher returns *and* higher returns per unit of manufacturing time. It makes no sense to invest time in the cheaper technology 1, which produces lower returns *and* lower returns per unit of manufacturing time.

So let's try a final problem set (Table 4.4).

Table 4.4. Example Data

	Technology 1	Technology 2
Manufacturing time (hr) m	$m_1 = 3$	$m_2 = 6$
Procurement rate (kcal/hr) r	$r_1 = 2$	$r_2 = 3$
r / m	$r_1 / m_1 = .67$	$r_2 / m_2 = .50$

Let's check the conditions first this time. In this instance the more costly technology 2 produces higher returns (3 > 2), and the lower return technology 1 produces at least equivalent returns per unit of manufacturing time (.67 > .50). So we're all okay: the cheap and costly technologies are potentially competitive. Now plug the values into the equation for $s_{1\leftrightarrow2}$:

$$s_{1\leftrightarrow2} = (r_1m_2 - r_2m_1) / (r_2 - r_1)$$

$$= (2{*}6 - 3{*}3) / (3 - 2)$$

$$= (12 - 9) / (1)$$

$$= 3 / 1$$

$$= 3$$

And to be doubly sure, let's see whether the two technologies produce the same results at the critical procurement time switching point $s_{1 \leftrightarrow 2}$ = 3. And sure enough:

$$r_2 / (m_2 + s_{1 \leftrightarrow 2}) = r_1 / (m_1 + s_{1 \leftrightarrow 2})$$

$$3 / (6 + 3) = 2 / (3 + 3)$$

$$3 / 9 = 2 / 6$$

$$.33 = .33$$

Translated into plain English, $s_{1 \leftrightarrow 2}$ is a critical procurement time threshold, above which the more costly technology is superior and below which the cheaper technology is superior. And we learned what we already knew—that the more time one spends doing something, in this case procuring resources, the more it pays to invest in costly technologies that produce higher returns.

End of lesson? Well, not quite. It turns out this model can be directly applied to a very different kind of problem that hunters and gatherers always faced when operating some distance away from their home base. Think about it this way: you're getting two models for the price of one!

FIELD PROCESSING I

UTAH, Great Salt Lake shore, east of Lakeside Mountains, July. Heavy winds have blown a bumper crop of migratory grasshoppers (*Melanoplus sanguinipes*) into the lake, along the margins of which they have accumulated in vast, wave-heaped windrows. Attracted to this lucky windfall as a source of storable winter food, Skull Valley Gosiute living on the west side of the Lakeside Mountains travel back and forth between lakeshore and village, their conical carrying baskets filled with grasshoppers. But there's a problem. Grasshoppers have substantial food value as measured in kcal, but they also have chitinous exoskeletons that are indigestible and useless as food. A basket load of intact grasshoppers contains a substantial fraction of this useless chitin, which takes up valuable load space and weight. A carrying basket of grasshoppers from which the legs, wings, and miscellaneous other chitinous parts have been removed contains substantially less waste, thus more kcal, but removing these parts takes time (think about peeled shrimp).

The hunter-gatherers assembled on the Great Salt Lake shore thus weigh the alternatives. On the one hand, carrying unprocessed grasshoppers from lakeshore to village takes less time per basket load than carrying processed grasshoppers. On the other hand, however, a basket load of unprocessed grasshoppers contains fewer kcal than a basket load of processed grasshoppers. Which is the better choice? The *field process - ing model* described below is designed to address this sort of trade-off.

Introduction

Field processing falls under the larger heading of central place foraging, a family of situations in which foragers acquire things that have utility (e.g., prey, toolstone, firewood) at some distance from a central place where they are needed. Unlike diet breadth, where the problem is maximizing the rate at which this utility is acquired, the central place problem is maximizing the rate at which it is moved from the field to a central place. Put another way, in diet breadth the idea is "Get utility"; in central place foraging the idea is "Go out, get utility, bring it back."

In field processing, transport is limited by load size—the maximum load a forager can carry—which puts a premium on load quality. Field processing produces higher quality loads, offering potentially greater transport ("bring it back") efficiency. Note that efficiency matters only to the extent that transport is involved: no transport, no processing, no problem. In field processing, then, transport cost—specifically roundtrip travel time to and from the field location—is the critical variable. We know the rate at which resources are acquired and the rate at which processing increases load utility. What we want to know is how far the load has to be transported to justify taking the extra time to reduce the resource to this higher quality load. If processing is very time consuming and the distance between field location and central place is very small, it will generally make more sense to transport the resource unprocessed. If, on the other hand, field location and central place are far apart and the value of an unprocessed load is low, it will often make sense to improve transport efficiency by processing the resource to make a higher quality load.

In this case we are modeling field processing as a contingency problem, the either-or choice being "process all" or "process none." We are not permitting foragers the choice of a mixed load—some processed, some not—a situation more appropriate to linear programming (see Chapter 2). At the same time, as in linear programming, important external constraints—the maximum load the forager can carry—are imposed from the start. Without that constraint, of course, there would be no need to field process the resource; just like Hercules, foragers would simply carry the whole of the available resource home without processing. Not being Hercules, however, foragers need to know whether it will be in their interest to field process the resource into a higher utility load.

We are discussing field processing at this juncture because, as will shortly be made clear, the field processing model developed below is formally identical to the technological investment model developed above. This close relationship provides a solid foundation for introducing the general problem of field processing, stating it in a familiar, generic form rather than one specifically designed for field processing. With this introduction you will have no problem mastering the equally simple model specifically designed for field processing problems presented in Chapter 5.

The Generic Model

Let's start with the key variables and their symbols.

f_i Foraging time: the amount of time expended to obtain and process a resource—f_1 being the time required to obtain a full unprocessed load, f_2 the time to both obtain *and field process* a higher quality load of the same size.

u_i Utility: the value of the package—u_1 being the utility of the unprocessed load, u_2 the utility of the processed load expressed in kcal (i.e., kcal/load).

t Travel time: the total amount of time spent traveling to and from the kill site (i.e., roundtrip).

The relationship between this problem and that of technological investment is obvious from Figure 4.5, which shows that the problem of field processing is formally identical to the problem of technological investment (see Figure 4.4). As shown in Table 4.5, the variables that operationalize the field processing model are simply substitutes for those used in the technological investment model.

A second similarity between technological investment and field processing is that processed and unprocessed loads are viable alternatives only when they satisfy conditions equivalent to those required for alternative technologies.

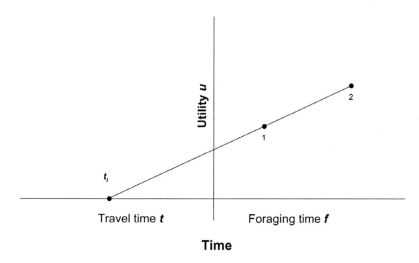

Figure 4.5. Foraging time and utility per load with (2) and without (1) field processing a resource. At the roundtrip travel time t_i, the return rates with and without processing are identical. Note the similarity of this problem to the one depicted in Figure 4.4.

Condition 1. The processed load must have higher utility.

Obviously field processing must increase utility. Formally:

$$\text{if } f_2 > f_1, \text{ then } u_2 > u_1$$

Condition 2. The unprocessed load must generate at least equivalent utility per unit of foraging time.

Since processed loads have higher utility, it makes no sense *not* to process unless unprocessed loads are competitive in terms of utility per unit of foraging time. Formally:

$$\text{if } u_1 < u_2, \text{ then } u_1 / f_1 \geq u_2 / f_2$$

As in the technological investment model, if utility is maximized only in relation to foraging time, field processing will only make sense in the special case $u_1 / f_1 = u_2 / f_2$ (i.e., processing and not processing generate equal utility per unit of foraging time). If $u_1 / f_1 > u_2 / f_2$, field processing will only make sense if load utility is maximized in relation to foraging and other time costs the forager must incur, most notably roundtrip travel time—the time spent traveling to and from the foraging location. The role of travel time here is the same as that of procurement time in the technological investment model. When processing and not processing are

Table 4.5. Relationship Between Technological Investment and Field Processing Models

Technological investment				Field processing
Manufacturing time (hr)	m	replaced by	f	Foraging time (hr)
Procurement rate (kcal/hr)	r	replaced by	u	Utility (kcal/load)
Procurement time (hr)	s	replaced by	t	Travel time (hr)

both potentially viable, it is roundtrip travel time that ultimately determines whether foragers should take time to process and transport a higher quality load. The travel time needed to make field processing worthwhile is given by the *travel time switching point*, which is computed in exactly the same way that the *procurement time switching point* is calculated in technological investment.

Procurement time switching point: $s_{1 \leftrightarrow 2} = (r_1 m_2 - r_2 m_1) / (r_2 - r_1)$

Travel time switching point: $t_{1 \leftrightarrow 2} = (u_1 f_2 - u_2 f_1) / (u_2 - u_1)$

You can prove this for yourself by using the equation used earlier to solve for procurement switching time in the technological investment model (Appendix 4). As spelled out in Appendix 5, simply substitute the terms for field processing—that is, for m substitute f, for r substitute u, and for s substitute t.

Technological investment: $r_2 / (m_2 + s) = r_1 / (m_1 + s)$

Field processing: $u_2 / (f_2 + t) = u_1 / (f_1 + t)$

So let's try an example. Suppose it takes our Great Salt Lake foragers 3 hours to fill a basket load of unprocessed grasshoppers worth 40,000 kcal, and 7 hours for a load of processed grasshoppers worth 80,000 kcal. How far do our foragers have to be from camp to justify adding the 4 hours needed to obtain a processed load? The values just described are those in Table 4.6.

Before we go any further, we need to know whether processing and not processing are potentially viable alternatives according to the conditions previously stated. As it turns out, they are. The more costly processed load has higher utility (80,000 > 40,000). The less costly unprocessed load has at least equivalent utility relative to foraging time (13,333.33 > 11,428.57).

Table 4.6. Example Data

	No processing	Processing
Foraging time (hr) f	$f_1 = 3$	$f_2 = 7$
Utility (kcal) u	$u_1 = 40{,}000$	$u_2 = 80{,}000$
u/f	$u_1/f_1 = 13333.33$	$u_2/f_2 = 11428.57$

All we have to do to calculate the travel time switching point (between not processing and processing) is plug our given values into the equation for $t_{1 \leftrightarrow 2}$:

$$t_{1 \leftrightarrow 2} \quad = (u_1 f_2 - u_2 f_1) / (u_2 - u_1)$$

$$= (40{,}000*7 - 80{,}000*3) / (80{,}000 - 40{,}000)$$

$$= (280{,}000 - 240{,}000) / (40{,}000)$$

$$= 40{,}000 / 40{,}000$$

$$= 1$$

That is, if the roundtrip travel time between foragers and their camp is greater than 1 hour, they should field process and carry home the higher value 80,000-kcal load. To make sure, let's see whether not processing and processing produce the same results at the critical foraging time switching point $t_{1 \leftrightarrow 2} = 1$:

$$u_2 / (f_2 + t_{1 \leftrightarrow 2}) = u_1 / (f_1 + t_{1 \leftrightarrow 2})$$

And indeed they do:

$$u_2 / (f_2 + t_{1 \leftrightarrow 2}) = u_1 / (f_1 + t_{1 \leftrightarrow 2})$$

$$80{,}000 / (7 + 1) = 40{,}000 / (3 + 1)$$

$$80{,}000 / 8 = 40{,}000 / 4$$

$$10{,}000 = 10{,}000$$

One good thing about the field processing model is that we can use it to solve for any two successive stages of processing. For instance, in the example we've been using so far, the travel time switching point from no processing to processing is given by the equation:

$$t_{1 \leftrightarrow 2} = (u_1 f_2 - u_2 f_1) / (u_2 - u_1)$$

Suppose Great Salt Lake foragers could carry still more grasshopper kcal home if the cleaned grasshoppers were made lighter by drying — the cumulative time needed to procure, clean, and dry a load being f_3 and the utility of the cleaned and dried load being u_3. Assuming that grasshopper drying is a viable option (i.e., $f_3 > f_2$ but $u_3 > u_2$; $u_2 < u_3$ but $u_2 / f_2 \geq u_3 / f_3$), the travel time switching point from cleaning to cleaning and drying is given by virtually the same equation as before:

$$t_{2 \leftrightarrow 3} = (u_2 f_3 - u_3 f_2) / (u_3 - u_2)$$

More generally the travel time switching point from any processing stage j-1 to another more intensive stage of processing j is given by the equation:

$$t_{j\text{-}1 \leftrightarrow j} = (u_{j\text{-}1} f_j - u_j f_{j\text{-}1}) / (u_j - u_{j\text{-}1}) \qquad \text{where}$$

$f_{j\text{-}1}$ is foraging time (procurement and processing) for the less processed stage

f_j is foraging time for the more processed stage

$u_{j\text{-}1}$ is utility at the less processed stage

u_j is utility at the more processed stage (again assuming $u_j > u_{j\text{-}1}$ and $f_j > f_{j\text{-}1}$)

As Figure 4.6 shows, the roundtrip travel time switching point increases for each additional processing stage. That is, as in the technological investment model, where more procurement time was required to justify more costly procurement technology, in field processing more travel time is required to justify more thorough processing. The roundtrip travel time switching point also increases if load size (hence utility) increases, as demonstrated in Exercises 4.5 and 4.6.

With that we're done! Well, I'm done. You're not: you have some exercises waiting.

FURTHER READING

Technological Investment

Bettinger, R. L., B. Winterhalder, and R. McElreath. (2006). A Simple Model of Technological Intensification. *Journal of Archaeological Science* 33:538–545.

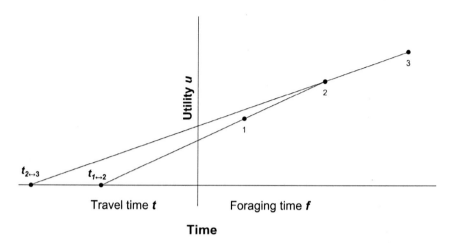

Figure 4.6. Roundtrip travel time switching point increases for each additional processing stage.

The original publication of the technological investment model outlined in this chapter. In this paper, and also in the Ugan, Bright, and Rogers (2003) reference given below, rate of return r is given as $f(m)$, reflecting that return rate is a function of cost. The original version is more correct but the one used here is simpler to follow.

Ugan, A., J. Bright, and A. Rogers. (2003). When Is Technology Worth the Trouble? *Journal of Archaeological Science* 30:1315–1329.
    The simple model of technological investment described in this chapter and in Bettinger, Winterhalder, and McElrath (2006) is a response to this paper, which assumed that procurement rate r increases at a constantly diminishing rate relative to manufacturing time m, describing a continuous asymptotic curve. While that assumption is certainly wrong, this paper is well worth reading.

Field Processing

Metcalfe, D., and K. R. Barlow. (1992). A Model for Exploring the Optimal Trade-off Between Field Processing and Transport. *American Anthropologist* 94:340–356.
    Probably the first anthropological application of the generic field processing model described in this chapter.

EXERCISES FOR CHAPTER 4

4.1. Determine whether the five pairs of technologies in Table 4.7 are mutually competitive and indicate the basis of your determination.

4.2. Determine the procurement time switching point $s_{1\leftrightarrow2}$ for the fifth pair of technologies in Table 4.7 (i.e., Pair 5).

4.3. Show that the fifth pair of technologies, for which you obtained the procurement time switching point in Exercise 4.2, produces exactly the same return at that switching time.

4.4. Table 4.8 provides foraging times and utilities obtained with and without field processing for two cases. For each case determine whether "no field processing" and "field processing" are mutually viable alternatives.

4.5. For Case 1 in Table 4.8:

4.5A. Determine the travel time switching point $t_{1\leftrightarrow2}$ for no processing and processing.

4.5B. Show that no processing and processing produce exactly the same returns at that travel time switching point.

Table 4.7. Data for Problems 4.1–4.3

Pair	Times and rates	Technology 1	Technology 2
1	Manufacturing time (hr) m	$m_1 = 8$	$m_2 = 10$
	Procurement rate (kcal/hr) r	$r_1 = 3$	$r_2 = 3$
	r/m	$r_1/m_1 = .38$	$r_2/m_2 = .30$
2	Manufacturing time (hr) m	$m_1 = 8$	$m_2 = 8$
	Procurement rate (kcal/hr) r	$r_1 = 3$	$r_2 = 4$
	r/m	$r_1/m_1 = .38$	$r_2/m_2 = .50$
3	Manufacturing time (hr) m	$m_1 = 8$	$m_2 = 10$
	Procurement rate (kcal/hr) r	$r_1 = 3$	$r_2 = 4$
	r/m	$r_1/m_1 = .38$	$r_2/m_2 = .40$
4	Manufacturing time (hr) m	$m_1 = 5$	$m_2 = 10$
	Procurement rate (kcal/hr) r	$r_1 = 3$	$r_2 = 4$
	r/m	$r_1/m_1 = .60$	$r_2/m_2 = .40$
5	Manufacturing time (hr) m	$m_1 = 3$	$m_2 = 10$
	Procurement rate (kcal/hr) r	$r_1 = 2$	$r_2 = 3$
	r/m	$r_1/m_1 = .67$	$r_2/m_2 = .30$

Table 4.8. Data for Problems 4.4–4.6

Case	Times and rates	No field processing	Field processing
1	Foraging time (hr) f	$f_1 = 1$	$f_2 = 8$
	Utility (kcal) u	$u_1 = 100$	$u_2 = 200$
	u / f (kcal/hr)	$u_1 / f_1 = 100$	$u_2 / f_2 = 25$
		no processing	processing
2	Foraging time (hr) f	$f_1 = 1.5$	$f_2 = 12.0$
	Utility (kcal) u	$u_1 = 150$	$u_2 = 300$
	u / f (kcal/hr)	$u_1 / f_1 = 100$	$u_2 / f_2 = 25$

4.6. In Table 4.8, Case 2 is designed to show what happens to the travel time switching point as load size increases, in this instance giving a forager the ability to carry a load half again larger than was assumed in Case 1. In Case 2 utility with *no processing* increases by 50%, from 100 kcal to 150 kcal, and with it foraging time because the forager is filling a larger load. Utility and foraging time *with processing* likewise increase by 50%. Keeping in mind that nothing but load size has increased:

4.6A. Calculate the travel time switching point for no processing and processing for Case 2. If you do this right, you will get a value for $t_{1\leftrightarrow2}$ that is larger than that obtained for Case 1 because load size has increased.

4.6B. Finally, show that *no processing* and *processing* produce exactly the same returns at the travel time switching point you obtained for Case 2.

4.7. The last exercises deal with a real archaeological problem. David Zeanah (2000, Transport Costs, Central-Place Foraging, and Hunter-Gatherer Alpine Land-Use Strategies, in *Intermountain Archaeology*, edited by D. B. Madsen and M. D. Metcalfe, pp. 1–14, University of Utah Anthropological Papers No. 122, Salt Lake City) has considered the problem of field processing mountain sheep (*Ovis canadensis*), which are too large to be carried by a single hunter even when butchered. He argues that hunters would likely circumvent this problem by drying mountain sheep meat. Freshly butchered meat has about 1258 kcal/kg and dried meat about 2013 kcal/kg. It takes about 10 hours to dry a full load of meat, which is 30 kilograms. If it takes a hunter 2 hours to kill a mountain sheep, how far in roundtrip travel time does the hunter have to be from home to justify drying a full load of meat? (Hint. Note that drying time is a special kind of processing because it does not vary in an obvious way with load size. It takes as much time to dry 1 kilogram as it does 30 kilograms cut into 1-kilogram packages. Thus you must solve this problem for the whole 30-kilogram load; you cannot solve it for 1 kilogram and multiply that value by load size.)

4.8. In the problem above, Zeanah was interested in a situation that had hunters living in a base camp on the floor of Owens Valley, California, and hunting in the White Mountains 27 kilometers away (a 54-kilometer roundtrip). Because we know the distance in question, we can restate the travel time threshold in terms of critical average walking speed — the average walking speed faster than which processing would not, and slower than which it would, be justified. Given this:

4.8A. What is the critical walking speed switching point?

4.8B. Zeanah argued that hunters traveled at 3 km/hr. Does this walking speed justify drying mountain sheep meat in the White Mountains?

ANSWERS TO CHAPTER 4 EXERCISES

4.1. Pair 1 not mutually competitive: the more costly technology does not produce higher returns. Pair 2 not mutually competitive: the lower return technology does not produce at least equivalent returns per unit of manufacturing time. Pair 3 not mutually competitive: the lower return technology does not produce at least equivalent returns per unit of manufacturing time. Pair 4 mutually competitive: more costly technology produces higher returns, less productive technology produces at least equivalent returns relative to manufacturing time. Pair 5 mutually competitive: more costly technology produces higher returns, less productive technology produces at least equivalent returns relative to manufacturing time.

4.2. $s_{1 \leftrightarrow 2}$ $= 11$

$$= (r_1 m_2 - r_2 m_1) / (r_2 - r_1)$$

$$= (2{*}10 - 3{*}3) / (3 - 2)$$

$$= (20 - 9) / (1)$$

$$= 11 / 1$$

$$= 11$$

4.3. $r_2 / (m_2 + s_{1 \leftrightarrow 2})$ $= r_1 / (m_1 + s_{1 \leftrightarrow 2})$

$3 / (10 + 11)$ $= 2 / (3 + 11)$

$3 / 21$ $= 2 / 14$

$1 / 7$ $= 1 / 7$

4.4. In both cases processing and not processing are mutually viable alternatives. Higher cost "field processing" produces higher returns. Lower return "no field processing" produces at least equivalent returns per unit of foraging time.

4.5A. $t_{1\leftrightarrow2}$ = 6

$$= (u_1f_2 - u_2f_1) / (u_2 - u_1)$$

$$= (100*8 - 200*1) / (200 - 100)$$

$$= (800 - 200) / (100)$$

$$= 600 / 100$$

$$= 6$$

4.5B. $u_2 / (f_2 + t_{1\leftrightarrow2})$ $= u_1 / (f_1 + t_{1\leftrightarrow2})$

$200 / (8 + 6)$ $= 100 / (1 + 6)$

$200 / 14$ $= 100 / 7$

14.29 $= 14.29$

4.6A. $t_{1\leftrightarrow2}$ = 9

$$= (u_1f_2 - u_2f_1) / (u_2 - u_1)$$

$$= (150*12 - 300*1.5) / (300 - 150)$$

$$= (1800 - 450) / (150)$$

$$= 1350 / 150$$

$$= 9$$

4.6B. $u_2 / (f_2 + t_{1\leftrightarrow2})$ $= u_1 / (f_1 + t_{1\leftrightarrow2})$

$300 / (12 + 9)$ $= 150 / (1.50 + 9)$

$300 / 21$ $= 150 / 10.50$

14.29 $= 14.29$

4.7. $t_{1\leftrightarrow2}$ = 14.66 hr

        u_1 = 1258 kcal/kg x 30 kg = 37,740 kcal

        u_2 = 2013 kcal/kg x 30 kg = 60,390 kcal

        f_1 = 2 hr

        f_2 = 2 + 10 = 12 hr

        $t_{1\leftrightarrow2}$ = $(u_1f_2 - u_2f_1) / (u_2 - u_1)$

                = (37,740*12 – 60,390*2) / (60,390 – 37,740)

                = (452,880 – 120,780) / 22,650

                = 332,100 / 22,650

                = 14.66 hr

4.8A. 54 km / 14.66 hr = 3.68 km/hr. That is, if hunters walk at 3.68 km/hr, drying and not drying meat would produce exactly the same return.

4.8B. Yes, because the critical 3.68 km/hr is greater than 3 km/hr, the speed at which hunters actually walk. At a walking speed of 3 km/hr, the roundtrip travel time would be 18 hours, above the critical 14.66 hours needed to justify meat drying.

CHAPTER 5

FIELD PROCESSING II

NEVADA, Tosawi chert quarry, August. A hunter has veered a little off his course home from a successful foray for mountain sheep (*Ovis canadensis*) to visit the well-known Tosawi ("white" + "knife") chert quarry north of the Humboldt River. With his camp supply of toolstone running low, he wants to obtain as much of this splendid raw material as he can carry. Pushed to it he can manage about 50 kilograms, but he's already packing 40 kilograms of dried sheep meat, leaving room for just 10 kilograms of chert. While relatively abundant, the best raw material takes some time to find, and the greater part of most chunks will have to be trimmed away to fashion the bifaces he needs to keep his hunting kit in shape. Thus carrying home raw chunks means carrying home a lot of useless material. Further, although he's a good knapper, he does make mistakes and sometimes ruins perfectly good chunks—which, if he does his flaking at home, will also end up as useless transported material. Choosing to do some or all of his flaking at the quarry will obviously mean that he can carry home a 10-kilogram load of higher utility, and just as obviously require more on-site knapping time. Our hunter obsessively insists on carrying homogeneous loads, all unprocessed or processed to the same stage, making this a contingency problem. How should the hunter weigh alternate contingencies to devise the right course of action?

INTRODUCTION

The generic field processing model developed in Chapter 4 could be applied to the chert processing problem above, but doing so would require substantial information. Specifically, one would need to know the load utilities and on-site foraging times (procurement plus any processing time) for each of the possible transport alternatives: all raw material, all chunks with cortex removed, all chunks reduced to 1st stage (roughed

out) bifaces, and so on. This is because the generic field processing model
is, well, generic. As we have seen, we can apply exactly the same kind of
model to the problem of technological investment merely by changing
terms.

That nothing about the generic field processing model is unique to the
problem of field processing means the data must do all the work; the data
alone are telling us things specific to field processing. It is possible to con-
struct a less data-demanding model, specifically designed for the problem
of field processing, by making some basic assumptions about resources
and mutual relationships among utility, procurement, and processing.
The generic field processing model is data demanding precisely because
it makes no such assumptions.

THE MODEL

Insofar as variables are concerned, the only difference between the generic model of field processing and this one is that foraging time (i.e., in-field
time) is partitioned to distinguish procurement time s from processing
time p. This gives us the following variables.

s Procurement time: the time expended obtaining a resource — s_{j-1}
being the procurement time required for a load before being
processed to stage j (e.g., raw chert chunks), s_j the procurement
time for a load processed to stage j (e.g., chert biface blanks).

p Processing time: the time required to process a load — p_{j-1} being
the processing time required for condition or stage $j-1$ (e.g., biface
blanks), p_j the time required for processing to stage j.

u Utility: the value of the load — u_{j-1} being the utility of a load before
processing to stage j, u_j the utility of a load processed to stage j.

t Roundtrip travel time: the total amount of time spent traveling to
and from the foraging location.

Assumptions

The core of this model lies in our assumptions about these variables and
their relationships. The first assumption is that resources come in sizes or
amounts that permit foragers to procure *exactly* the weight or volume of
the resource they want; a forager who wants 10 kilograms of a resource
can obtain exactly 10 kilograms, or an average of exactly 10 kilograms
when the target quantity is 10 kilograms. This assumption holds for
many — if not most — resources of the kind we're interested in (e.g., grass
seeds, acorns, salmon, chert); where it doesn't, the model we're develop-

ing on the assumption that it does can be adjusted to take this into account, as we'll see later on.

The second assumption is that the rate at which a resource is procured is unaffected by amounts of procurement up to and including those required for a completely processed load. This is a fancy way of saying that rate of procurement does not change over the span of an individual foraging bout, which is what we're modeling. Again, this assumption seems reasonable for most resources, and where it doesn't the model can be adjusted.

The third assumption (more a definition) is that processing increases resource utility per unit of weight or volume inversely with the proportional decrease in resource weight or volume — that is, the weight (or volume) after processing as a fraction of weight (or volume) before processing. Let's be very specific about this relationship:

$$u_{after} = u_{before} \times wt_{before} / wt_{after} \qquad \text{or}$$

$$= u_{before} \times vol_{before} / vol_{after} \qquad \text{where}$$

u_{after} is utility per unit of weight (or volume) after

u_{before} is utility per unit of weight (or volume) before

wt_{before} is weight before

wt_{after} is weight after

vol_{before} is volume before

vol_{after} is volume after

For example, processing that halves weight doubles per-unit utility (i.e., by a factor of $1 / .50 = 2$). And again, processing that cuts volume by a third increases per-unit utility by 50% (by a factor of $1 / .67 = 1.50$). Confused? This example may help.

You have a 10 kilogram-load of ore that contains 1 kilogram of gold. You carefully pick out 5 kilograms of field rock, leaving 5 kilograms containing 1 kilogram of gold. Weight is halved and per unit utility is doubled from 1 kg gold / 10 kg ore to 1 kg gold / 5 kg ore. There may be some but I cannot think of any examples of field processing that would violate this assumption. In any case field processing that decreases utility is not permitted. Suppose, how-ever, you sometimes mistake gold for field rock and end up discarding .10 kilograms of gold, so that your 5-kilogram load has only .90 kilograms of gold. Doesn't this decrease utility? No. Assuming processing always results in such mistakes, the real utility before you started picking through the load was only .90 kilograms rather than 1 kilogram of gold, because somewhere along the line processing would eliminate .10 kilograms of gold. So now utility before is .90 kg gold / 10 kg ore, and utility after is .90 kg gold / 5 kg ore, still amounting to doubling of per-unit utility. Put another way, from start to finish the only utility that counts is the utility that remains when the resource is processed to its final state.

Our third assumption has an important corollary: as it increases utility, processing also increases the time that must be spent in all prior stages of procurement and processing. This is easiest to see in relation to procurement. If our flint knapper intends to carry unprocessed chert home from the Tosawi quarry, he will cease procuring chert as soon as he has found as much raw material as he can carry. What happens, however, if just before leaving he changes his mind and decides he wants to carry home more valuable biface blanks, and accordingly detaches useless cortex and a few large shaping flakes and in the process also discards flawed nodules from his existing load? Obviously he will end up with less than a full load and have to find more chert, and reduce *that* into blanks, until he ends up with a full load (Figure 5.1).

The key insight now is that procurement time with and without processing (s_j and s_{j-1}) and utility with and without processing (u_j and u_{j-1}) are directly proportional. To see this, first imagine the utility by weight is .50 for raw Tosawi chert and 1.00 for the more fully processed chert biface

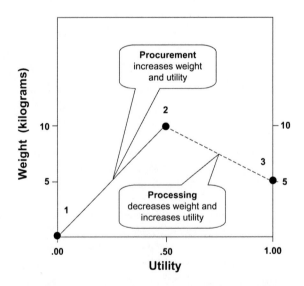

Figure 5.1. What happens when resources are processed. Forager starts with nothing (1), acquires a full 10-kilogram load (2), and doubles the utility of the resource by field processing (3), ending up with 5 kilograms, which is less than a full load. To carry home a full load of the higher quality, more fully processed product, another 10 kilograms of the resource must now be acquired and processed.

blanks. This means a 10-kilogram load of raw chert has the same utility as a 5-kilogram load of chert blanks (i.e., 10 kilograms @ .50 utility = 5 kilograms @ 1.00 utility). That is, in doubling the utility of chert, the flint knapper is halving its original (raw) weight. And if chert weight is halved, the knapper must spend twice as much time finding enough chert that, when flaked into blanks, will make a load; otherwise the load he carries home is half the size it should be, wasting valuable load capacity and thus transport time. In short, procurement time *with processing* is a function of (a) procurement time without processing *and* (b) the gain in utility that results from processing, just so:

$$s_j \,/\, s_{j-1} \;=\; u_j \,/\, u_{j-1}$$

$$s_j \qquad = s_{j-1}(u_j \,/\, u_j)$$

And plugging in the values from the above example (utility raw chert = .50, utility chert blanks = 1) gives:

$$s_j \qquad = s_{j-1}(u_j \,/\, u_{j-1})$$

$$\qquad = s_{j-1}(1 \,/.\, 50)$$

$$\qquad = 2s_{j-1}$$

Translated into plain English, this says that if the utility of raw chert is .50 and chert biface blanks is 1.00, the knapper who processes his chert into biface blanks will need to spend twice as much time finding chert as he would were he content to carry home raw chert, or $s_j = 2s_{j-1}$.

Let's try another example just to make sure we understand what's going on. Suppose the utility of whole pinenuts is .25 and that of hulled pinenuts is .75 (note the resemblance here to the linear programming problem discussed in Chapter 2). If it takes 1 hour to fill a 15-liter pack basket with nuts still in the shell, how long will it take to gather enough nuts that, when processed, will fill the 15-liter basket? Note that in this example we give the load constraint in volume rather than weight. It turns out this doesn't affect the results at all as long as utility is calculated relative to the measure in which load capacity is given (e.g., don't measure utility by weight when load capacity is measured by volume). So the answer is easy:

$$s_j \qquad = s_{j-1}(u_j \,/\, u_{j-1})$$

$$= 1 \text{ hr } (.75 \,/\, .25)$$

$$= 3 \text{ hr}$$

Again, this says that if the utility of whole pinenuts is 25% and that of hulled pinenuts is 75%, and if it takes 1 hour to acquire a load of whole nuts, it will take 3 hours to gather enough nuts that, when processed, will make a load. Pretty simple, huh?

Processing has the same multiplying effect on any prior stage of processing, increasing it by a factor of u_j / u_{j-1}. Suppose that starting from scratch, it takes 1 hour to knap a 10-kilogram load of 1st stage bifaces whose utility is one-third (.33) and 1 hour to reduce enough 1st stage bifaces to fill a 10-kilogram load of 2nd stage bifaces whose utility is one-half (.50). It follows that to complete a full load of 2nd stage bifaces will require 1.50 hours of processing 1st stage bifaces (1 hour 1st stage x .50 / .33 = 1.50 hour 1st stage).

Still confused? Figure 5.2 provides a more intuitively accessible rendering that may help clarify all these relationships. It illustrates the procurement and processing of a fat-rich nut (dark center) that is enclosed by a hard shell (inner ring), which is in turn enclosed by a husk (outer ring). Stage 1 processing removes the husk, Stage 2 the hard shell. The graphic depicts load constraint as a volume, reduced here to two dimensions, the areas shown being proportionally correct. If husk, shell, and nut density were identical, however, the constraint could be weight because the load space (area) taken up by the resource is the same regardless of processing stage. For skeptics Appendix 6 provides exact values for this example and its equivalent in three dimensions.

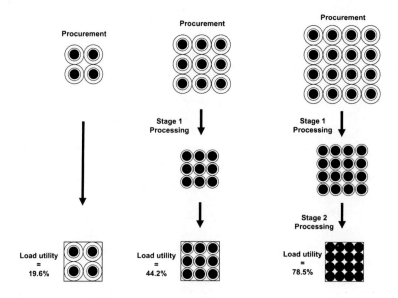

Figure 5.2. Graphic depiction of the procurement and processing of a small package resource, a fat-rich nut (black center) enclosed by a hard shell (inner ring), in turn enclosed by a husk (outer ring). The areas shown are proportionally correct. Stage 1 processing removes the husk, Stage 2 the hard shell.

Figure 5.2 makes it clear that each processing stage increases the amount of time that must be expended in all prior stages directly with the proportional gain in utility achieved by processing. Thus if 4 units of procurement time are required to obtain a full load of unprocessed nuts whose utility is 19.6%, 9 units of procurement time will be required if husks are removed to obtain a full load whose utility is 44.2% (4 x 44.20 / 19.60 = 9). Similarly, if 9 units of processing time are required to husk a full load of nuts whose utility is 44.2%, 16 units of husking time will be required to generate an amount of husked nuts that when shelled will make up a full load whose utility is 78.5% (9 x 78.50 / 44.20 = 16). By like reasoning, if 4 units of procurement time are required to obtain a full load of unprocessed nuts whose utility is 19.6%, it will take 16 units of procurement time to generate an amount of nuts that, when husked and shelled, will make up a full load whose utility is 78.5% (4 x 78.50 / 19.60 = 16). The same processing time is obtained if we consider just the two stages of processing. Thus if it takes 9 units of procurement time to generate a load of husked nuts with a utility of 44.2%, it will take 16 units of procurement time to generate a load of shelled nuts with a utility of 78.5% (9 x 78.50 / 44.20 = 16). See how easy it is?

Relationship Between Processing Time and Travel Time

Enough about procurement and processing time. What we really want to know is the relationship between processing and travel time—specifically, how large roundtrip travel time between field location and central place t must be to justify processing a resource into a higher quality load. It goes without saying (or it should) that, as in the generic model described in Chapter 4, processed and unprocessed loads are viable alternatives only when the processed load has higher utility or the unprocessed load generates at least equivalent utility per unit of foraging time. When they are, the critical travel threshold is obtained in the usual way—by determining the value of t at which processing and not processing end up transporting utility at exactly the same rate:

$$u_j / (s_j + p_j + t) = u_{j-1} / (s_{j-1} + t)$$

As shown in Appendix 7, solving for t gives:

$$t = p_j(u_{j-1} / [u_j - u_{j-1}])$$

Once again this value of t defines the critical *roundtrip travel time switching point* $t_{j-1 \leftrightarrow j}$ between not processing and processing:

$$t_{j-1 \leftrightarrow j} = p_j(u_{j-1} / [u_j - u_{j-1}])$$

Above this switching point—at greater roundtrip travel times ($t > t_{j\text{-}1\leftrightarrow j}$)—processing is favored, transporting utility more efficiently between field location and central place; below it, at lower roundtrip travel times ($t < t_{j\text{-}1\leftrightarrow j}$), the resource is more efficiently transported without processing (Figure 5.3).

To illustrate with reference to our chert example above (where the relative utility of raw chert $u_{j\text{-}1}$ is .50 and the utility of biface blanks u_j is 1), suppose it takes 1 hour to flake 2 kilograms of blanks, which is as much as we can carry, so p_j = 1 hr. According to the equation for $t_{j\text{-}1\leftrightarrow j}$, the critical roundtrip travel time switching point for the field processing of raw chert into blanks would then be 1 hour for this 2-kilogram load:

$$t_{j\text{-}1\leftrightarrow j} \quad = p_j(u_{j\text{-}1} / [u_j - u_{j\text{-}1}])$$

$$= 1 \text{ hr } (.50 / [1 - .50])$$

$$= 1 \text{ hr } (.50 / .50)$$

$$= 1 \text{ hr}$$

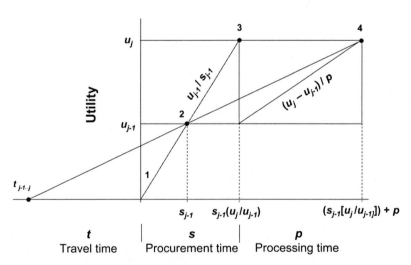

Figure 5.3. Field processing model. No Processing: Forager starts with nothing (1) and acquires a load of the unprocessed resource with utility $u_{j\text{-}1}$ (2). With Processing: Forager starts with nothing (1), acquires more than a full load of the resource (3), and processes that resource down into a full load of higher utility u_j (4). As explained in the text, if the forager requires procurement time $s_{j\text{-}1}$ for an unprocessed load, the time required to obtain enough resource to make a higher quality load will be $s_{j\text{-}1} (u_j / u_{j\text{-}1})$. When travel time is $t_{j\text{-}1\leftrightarrow j}$, no processing and processing produce exactly the same rate of return.

To see that this is the roundtrip travel time at which processing and not processing end up transporting utility at exactly the same rate, suppose it takes 1 hour to collect 2 kilograms of raw chert ($s_{j-1} = 1$). At the critical roundtrip travel time switching point of 1 hour, transporting a 2-kilogram load of raw chert (relatively utility = .50) will deliver the equivalent of 1 kilogram of useful chert every 2 hours (1 hour collecting + 1 hour traveling yields 2 kilograms of raw chert, half of it—or 1 kilogram—useful). If chert is reduced to biface blanks (relatively utility = 1) prior to transport, collecting time must increase from 1 hour to 2 hours to generate the 4 kilograms of raw chert needed to produce 2 kilograms of biface blanks: $s_j = s_{j-1}u_j / u_{i-j} = 1$ hr x 1 / .50 = 2 hr. Transporting the 2-kilogram load of biface blanks will then deliver 2 kilograms of useful chert every 4 hours (2 hours collecting + 1 hour processing + 1 hour traveling), which is exactly the rate at which useful chert is delivered without processing (2 kg / 4 hr with processing = 1 kg / 2 hr without processing).

Note that since processing time p_j and initial and final utility u_{j-1} and u_j are always positive, the travel time threshold $t_{j-1\oplus j}$ above which processing increases transport efficiency is always greater than zero ($t_j > 0$)—unless processing does not increase utility (i.e., $u_{j-1} \geq u_j$), in which case field processing would obviously be foolish regardless of travel time. Put another way, there is always some travel distance beyond which any kind of non-foolish processing (i.e., $u_j > u_{j-1}$) will make sense, and nearer than which it will not.

Role of Procurement Time

Perhaps the most interesting thing about the equation used to obtain $t_{j-1\oplus j}$ is this: it does not contain a term for procurement time, either with processing s_j or without processing s_{j-1}. Neither does it contain a term for prior processing time p_{j-1}. What does this mean? Well, think about it for a minute. It means procurement time has no bearing on the travel time switching point at which processing is favored. The travel time switching point is determined entirely by the utility of the resource immediately prior to processing, the time processing takes, and the increase in resource utility that results.

To see this with reference to the chert example we've been using, suppose that instead of 1 hour, it takes 3 hours to collect 2 kilograms of toolstone—the load size we're limited to. Then at the same 1-hour travel time switching point, transporting the 2-kilogram load of raw chert will deliver 1 kilogram of usable chert every 4 hours (3 hours collecting + 1 hour traveling = 2 kilograms of raw chert, half of it—or 1 kilogram—useful). On the other hand, if toolstone is transported as biface blanks, it will now take 6 hours to collect the requisite 4 kilograms of raw chert, and transporting biface blanks will deliver 2 kilograms of usable chert every 8 hours (6 hours collecting + 1 hour processing + 1 hour traveling = 2 kilograms of biface blanks, all of it useful), which is exactly the rate at which

usable chert is delivered without processing (2 kg / 8 hr with processing
= 1 kg / 4 hr without processing). The *roundtrip travel time switching point*
$t_{j-1 \leftrightarrow j}$ did not change even though foraging time — the time needed to find
2 kilograms of raw chert — increased threefold from 1 hour to 3 hours!

In sum, the rate at which resources are acquired has no effect on the
travel time switching point. As noted above, this means there is always a
travel time switching point even when acquisition rates are very low, as
shown in Figure 5.4.

That travel time switching points are constant has very important
ethnographic and archaeological implications. A good deal of contempo-
rary foraging research is aimed at determining return rates experimental-
ly. This is critical in diet breadth, for example, where resource ranking
depends on handling time rates, kcal/hr, or hr/kcal (see Chapter 1). To
figure this out, researchers actually harvest this or that resource to determine how much was harvested and its value in kcal, and use this to determine the relative ranking of different plants and animals. The archaeological value of this is obvious. Finding large quantities of low-ranking
resources (few kcal per unit of handling time) in an archaeological site
strongly indicates wide diet breadth, implying that resources were scarce
relative to demand.

Resource processing experiments (e.g., threshing, winnowing,
butchering, lithic reduction, etc.) are conducted with something similar in
mind. In theory, experiments with different forms of food and raw material processing permit us to infer how far people went to obtain the

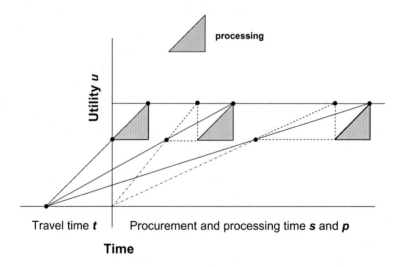

Figure 5.4. Effect of increasing procurement time on $t_{j-1 \leftrightarrow j}$. As procurement time
increases, from left to right, travel time switching point remains constant. There is
always a critical travel time switching point below which (at lesser roundtrip travel
times) processing will not be favored.

resources represented in archaeological sites. Thus finding large quantities of cortical chert flakes in a base camp says that the source of the chert was close by, that cortical reduction was very time consuming relative to the gain in utility, or some combination of the two. Conversely, chert quarries showing evidence of extensive lithic reduction were likely used by knappers a long way from home. Zooarchaeologists use the same logic to argue that residential camps with many low-utility skeletal elements signify hunting nearby, and kill sites lacking only very high-utility elements signify hunters coming from a distance.

The problem here is that if processing thresholds — roundtrip distance required to justify processing — hinged on (changed directly with) procurement rates, we would be unable to distinguish processing that is a response to travel time from processing that is a response to procurement rates. Consider the effect this would have on lithic reduction at a quarry used for thousands of years, gradually decreasing the amount of easily available raw material. Clearly, as procurement rates dropped over time, the amount of lithic reduction would increase because the travel time switching point required to justify different degrees of reduction would likewise decrease. The effect would be the same if instead procurement rates stayed the same but people gradually moved farther and farther from the quarry! Now you see the importance of our finding that processing thresholds are independent of procurement rate. People will hull pinenuts at some critical travel time switching point whether pinenuts are abundant or not. And we can determine these thresholds by experiment.

Discussion

A couple of other useful things to know. First, our use of $t_{j-1 \leftrightarrow j}$ is not limited to the simple dichotomy between processing and not processing. Rather, because (as noted above) the equation for $t_{j-1 \leftrightarrow j}$ contains no term for either procurement time s or prior processing time p_{j-1}, $t_{j-1 \leftrightarrow j}$ can be construed as *roundtrip travel time switching point* for *any* two successive stages in a procurement-processing sequence. For instance, take the following reduction sequence:

> raw chert → cortex removed → 1st shaping → 2nd shaping → final shaping

We can calculate $t_{j-1 \leftrightarrow j}$ for any two adjacent stages:

> raw chert → cortex removed

> cortex removed → 1st shaping

first shaping → 2nd shaping

2nd shaping → final shaping

Further, we can lump successive stages into larger stages as long as we keep them in sequence and omit no intervening steps:

raw chert & cortex removed & 1st shaping → 2nd shaping & final shaping

raw chert & cortex removed → 1st shaping & 2nd shaping & final shaping

raw chert & cortex removed & 1st shaping → 2nd shaping

cortex removed → 1st shaping & 2nd shaping

raw chert → cortex removed & 1st shaping & 2nd shaping & final shaping

We need only keep track of the final utility at each of the two stages u_{j-1} and u_j and the total processing time for the second stage. Final utility for a combined stage is simply the utility after the last step of that stage. For example, suppose we are calculating $t_{j-1 \leftrightarrow j}$ for the stages:

raw chert & cortex removed → 1st shaping & 2nd shaping

In this instance final utility for the first stage u_{j-1} is utility of chert after cortex is removed, and final utility for the second stage u_j is utility of chert after the 2nd round of shaping. The only place where you can really get confused is in calculating processing time for the second stage (processing time for the first stage doesn't matter, not entering the equation for $t_{j-1 \leftrightarrow j}$). Here *you must remember* that processing that increases utility not only increases procurement time; it also increases processing time for any earlier stage of processing. So when the second stage includes more than one step, you must adjust processing times accordingly. For example, suppose we want to determine $t_{j-1 \leftrightarrow j}$ for the two stages:

cortex removed → 1st shaping & 2nd shaping

Further, suppose the utilities and processing times are as given in Table 5.1.

Table 5.1 immediately provides two of the three values we need to determine $t_{j-1 \leftrightarrow j}$. One is u_{j-1} = .50, which is utility once cortex is removed;

Table 5.1. Utilities and Processing Times for a Two-Stage Chert Processing Problem (see text)

Process	First stage j-1	Second stage j	
	Cortex removed	1st shaping	2nd shaping
Processing time (hr)	—	$p_{j1st} = 1$	$p_{j2nd} = 1$
Utility	$u_{j-1} = .50$	$u_{j1st} = .75$	$u_{j2nd} = .80$

the other is $u_j = .80$, which is final utility at second stage u_{j2nd} (i.e., after 2nd shaping). Note that processing time for the first stage p_{j-1} isn't given because it doesn't matter; we don't need it to determine $t_{j-1\leftrightarrow j}$. We *do* need processing time for the second stage p_j, which is a bit tricky because it entails two separate processing steps (1st shaping and 2nd shaping), whose individual processing times we can label $p_{j1st} = 1$ hr and $p_{j2nd} = 1$ hr. One might think, then, that processing time for the second stage would be their sum (2 hours) but it's not. Remember, when a processing stage increases utility, it increases processing times for all prior stages. And it increases them directly in relative proportion to the utility gained by processing at the second stage.

In this case 1st shaping a full load of chert bifaces from cortex-free chunks takes 1 hour. If just that amount is further processed by 2nd shaping, increasing its utility from .75 to .80, it will no longer make up a full load; processing it by 2nd shaping will reduce the initial amount in weight (or volume, whichever limits load size) by a factor of u_{j1st} / u_{j2nd}, giving us about .94 (.75 / .80) of a load. This means if we want a full load of chert processed by 2nd shaping, we'll have to do more than 1 hour of 1st shaping. Specifically, for a full load, time given to 1st shaping will have to increase by a factor of u_{j2nd} / u_{j1st}. In short, processing time for this stage is not $p_j = p_{j1st} + p_{j2nd}$ but rather:

$$p_j = (p_{j1st}[u_{j2nd} / u_{j1st}]) + p_{j2nd}$$

$$= 1.00 \text{ hr } (.80 / .75) + 1.00 \text{ hr}$$

$$= 1.00 \text{ hr } (1.07) + 1.00 \text{ hr}$$

$$= 2.07 \text{ hr}$$

Plugging this value into the equation for the roundtrip travel time switching point $t_{j-1\leftrightarrow j}$ would then give:

$$t_{j-1\leftrightarrow j} \quad = p_j(u_{j-1} / [u_j - u_{j-1}])$$

$$= 2.07(.50 / (.80 - .50))$$

$$= 2.07(.50 / .30)$$

$$= 2.07(1.67)$$

$$= 3.45 \text{ hr}$$

If there were three processing steps within the stage, we would need to make the same adjustment twice. The first step would be to compute processing time for the first two substages when combined, exactly as above:

1st step: $p_{j1st\&2nd} = (p_{j1st}[u_{j2nd} / u_{j1st}]) + p_{j2nd}$

This would now leave us with two substages with known processing times, the first two when combined and the third. We would compute the total processing time for these two when combined following the same method:

2nd step: $p_{j1st\&2nd\&3rd} = (p_{j1st\&2nd}[u_{j3rd} / u_{j2nd}]) + p_{j3rd}$

Note here again that final utility for the combined substages 1st shaping & 2nd shaping is u_{j2nd}, utility after both steps are finished. By similar reasoning, the final utility for all three stages combined would be u_{j3rd}. We can combine as many stages as we like, using this same procedure successively.

A second useful thing to know has to do with how we measure utility. In the equation used to obtain $t_{j-1\leftrightarrow j}$, the terms for utility cancel each other out. This means we can calculate utility in any scale we choose. As long as our utility measure is in an interval scale, and the relationships are direct, everything will work out fine. Instead of absolute utility, for example, suppose we had calculated our chert problem in units of cutting edge—each kilogram of chert biface blanks having the equivalent of, say, 30 centimeters of cutting edge and raw chert having half that (15 centimeters). This gives us the very same travel time switching point we obtained originally:

$$t_{j-1\leftrightarrow j} \quad = p_j(u_{j-1} / [u_j - u_{j-1}])$$

$$= 1 \text{ hr } (15 \text{ cm} / [30 \text{ cm} - 15 \text{ cm}])$$

$$= 1 \text{ hr } (15 \text{ cm} / 15 \text{ cm})$$

$$= 1 \text{ hr}$$

And if instead chert biface blanks had the equivalent of 52 centimeters of cutting edge, we would still get the same result:

$$t_{j-1\leftrightarrow j} \quad = p_j(u_{j-1} \,/\, [u_j - u_{j-1}])$$

$$= 1 \text{ hr } (26 \text{ cm } / \, [52 \text{ cm } - 26 \text{ cm}])$$

$$= 1 \text{ hr } (26 \text{ cm } / \, 26 \text{ cm})$$

$$= 1 \text{ hr}$$

But enough of this. You get the idea.

My third and final point is about how we obtain processing time p_j for a single stage. In the chert example we've been using, we calculated processing time simply as the time to process a load of biface blanks, 1 hour for the 2-kilogram load. We might have just as easily determined the rate at which raw chert is reduced to biface blanks (.50 hr / kg) and multiplied that by load size (2 kilograms) to obtain the same 1-hour value. This seems pretty obvious—even trivial—and I mention it mainly because it so clearly demonstrates the effect that changing load size has on the *roundtrip travel time switching point* $t_{j-1\leftrightarrow j}$, which varies directly with load size: bigger loads means larger roundtrip travel time switching points. This makes sense given the logic of central place foraging: to move as much utility as quickly as possible from the field to central place. In this context, because field processing takes time, slowing down the whole process, it only makes sense because load size is limited—no limit, no processing. It follows, then, that the more we increase load capacity, the less justification there will be for taking time in the field to process a resource into a higher quality load.

Can you think of any obvious implications here? What happens to field processing when people domesticate beasts of burden? What about physical stature and strength? Clearly, if bigger, stronger people can carry larger loads, they will be less likely to process resources than smaller, weaker people. Wouldn't you think this probably means, other things being equal, that men are less likely to field process resources than women?

BIG PACKAGE RESOURCES

I mentioned at the outset that the model we've been developing could be modified to deal with resources that do not meet our first assumption that resources come in sizes or amounts that permit foragers to procure *exactly* the weight or volume of the resource they want. Can you think of any exceptions? I can.

VENEZUELA–BRAZIL BORDER, uplands. A Yanomamo hunter a long way from home comes upon and kills a 9-meter, 230-kilogram green anaconda (*Eunectes murinus*). Since he can only carry 50 kilograms, the Yanomamo hunter has two choices: (a) slice off a 50-kilogram hunk of the snake and head for home, or (b) slice off a larger hunk and process it into a higher quality load. Which is the best choice?

The anaconda represents what I call a *big package resource*, one that comes in sizes much larger than the forager can possibly carry even when fully processed. By contrast, the resources whose field processing we've been modeling can be termed *small package resources*, which—according to our first assumption—come in sizes that permit foragers to acquire them in exactly the quantity they want. The difference is critical because big package processing does not require additional procurement time. With the anaconda, since the kill has already been made and it takes no more time to slice off 100 kilograms for processing than it does to slice off 50 kilograms for immediate transport, processing adds no procurement time. Seen this way, procurement includes all the steps (and time) needed to ready an unprocessed load for immediate transport; anything after that is processing.

Of course the log-like anaconda is unusual. For most big packages, it will take more time to detach a larger portion than a smaller one. It's going to take more time to carve off 75 kilograms of mammoth meat for processing than it will to carve off 50 kilograms for immediate transport, for example. In such cases processing time includes only the additional increment needed to detach the larger portion, which makes sense from the perspective of the mammoth hunter. One way or the other, he's going to spend at least the time needed to carve off a 50-kilogram load for immediate transport, so the amount of time that takes is rightly written off as part of procurement. Any additional carving, however, is just as rightly charged to processing.

As so many times before, we obtain travel thresholds for big package resources by determining the value of roundtrip travel time t at which processing and not processing end up transporting utility at exactly the same rate:

$$u_j / (s + p_{j-1}[u_j / u_{j-1}] + p_j + t) = u_{j-1} / (s + p_{j-1} + t) \qquad \text{where}$$

p_j is time required to process a load to stage j

p_{j-1} is time required to process a load to stage $j-1$

u_{j-1} is load utility before processing to stage j

u_j is load utility after processing to stage j

t is roundtrip travel time

s is time required to procure a full, unprocessed load

As shown in Appendix 8, this gives us our required travel time switching point:

$$t_{j-1 \leftrightarrow j} = p_j(u_{j-1} / [u_j - u_{j-1}]) - s$$

You will note that the travel time switching point for processing big packages differs from that for small packages only by the subtraction of the term s, which is procurement time. The small package version does not contain the term for procurement time s, because (as we have seen) changes in procurement time do not affect small package processing thresholds. The big package version contains the term s, because changes in procurement time do affect big package foraging thresholds, which increase and decrease directly as a function of s. All else equal, big packages are more likely to be field processed than small packages; that is, their travel time switching points will be smaller.

To assure yourself that the equation above works for any stage of big package field processing, consider the data in Table 5.2, which describes a big package resource that takes 10 hours to procure and has a utility of .35. To process a load of this big package to the first stage takes another 10 hours, raising load utility to .60. Processing it to a second, more refined stage takes 12.50 hours of 1st stage processing (remember, here we need more product processed to Stage 1 because 2nd stage processing reduces load size) and another 10 hours of 2nd stage processing, raising load utility to .75.

Table 5.2. Data for a Big Package Processing Problem (see text)

	No Processing	Processing to 1st stage	Processing to 2nd stage
Utility	.35	.60	.75
Procurement (hr)	10.00	10.00	10.00
1st stage processing (hr)		10.00	12.50
2nd stage processing (hr)			10.00
Utility / hr	.035	.030	.023

Letting u_{j-1} be utility without processing, the travel time switching point for 1st stage processing is thus:

$$t_{j-1 \leftrightarrow j} \quad = p_j(u_{j-1} / [u_j - u_{j-1}]) - s$$

$$= 10.00(.35 / [.60 - .35]) - 10.00$$

$$= 10.00(.35 / .25) - 10.00$$

$$= 14.00 - 10.00$$

$$= 4.00$$

It's always wise to double-check that processing and not processing do in fact produce equivalent returns at $t_{j-1 \leftrightarrow j} = 4$, which indeed they do:

$u_j / (s + p_j + t)$	$= u_{j-1} / (s + t)$
.60 / (10.00 + 10.00 + 4.00)	= .35 / (10.00 + 4.00)
.60 / 24.00	= .35 / 14.00
.025	= .025

We determine the travel time switching point for 2nd stage processing in exactly the same way:

$$t_{j-1 \leftrightarrow j} \quad = p_j(u_{j-1} / [u_j - u_{j-1}]) - s$$

$$= 10.00(.60 / [.75 - .60]) - 10.00$$

$$= 10.00(.60 / .15) - 10.00$$

$$= 10.00(4.00) - 10.00$$

$$= 40.00 - 10.00$$

$$= 30.00$$

And again we double-check to show that at $t_{j-1 \leftrightarrow j} = 30.00$, processing to the 1st stage and processing to the 2nd stage produce exactly the same rate of return, which they do:

$$u_j / (s + p_{j-1}[u_j / u_{j-1}] + p_j + t) = u_{j-1} / (s + p_{j-1} + t)$$

.75 / (10.00 + 10.00[.75 / .60] +10.00 + 30.00) = .60 / (10.00 + 10.00 + 30.00)

.75 / (10.00 + 12.50 +10.00 + 30.00) = .60 / (10.00 + 10.00 + 30.00)

.75 / 62.50 = .60 / 50.00

.012 = .012

A GENERAL MODEL OF FIELD PROCESSING

Since we've come this far, it's worth thinking a little more deeply about what makes big package resources different from small package resources insofar as field processing is concerned. As we've just seen, their processing thresholds differ only in the term s for procurement time. This makes it possible to think of the big-small distinction not as a dichotomy but as a continuum. That is, we can modify the equation for big packages by multiplying the term for procurement time s by a coefficient e (where $e \leq 1$), giving:

$$t_{j-1 \leftrightarrow j} = p_j(u_{j-1} / [u_j - u_{j-1}]) - se$$

For big packages let $e = 1$, so:

$$t_{j-1 \leftrightarrow j} = p_j(u_{j-1} / [u_j - u_{j-1}]) - s$$

Similarly, for small packages let $e = 0$, so:

$$t_{j-1 \leftrightarrow j} = p_j(u_{j-1} / [u_j - u_{j-1}])$$

The interesting thing is that read this way, e need have nothing to do with the physical size of a resource. True, $e = 1$ for immensely large resources (anacondas, whales, mammoths, etc.). However, it is entirely possible that e will approach 1 for very small resources. For example, the windrowed grasshoppers used to illustrate field processing in Chapter 4 might be so concentrated that obtaining a larger load for processing would take negligibly more time than obtaining a smaller unprocessed load. Because of this, I think of e as a measure of resource concentration. Setting $e = 1$ implies a resource so densely concentrated that it takes no more time to procure the larger amount needed for a processed load than to procure the smaller amount for an unprocessed load. By contrast, setting $e = 0$ implies a resource sufficiently dispersed that procuring the larger amount takes just as much time per unit of resource as procuring the smaller amount—that is, that rate of procurement does not change as a function of procurement. Setting $0 < e < 1$ implies that it takes more time to procure the larger amount needed for a processed load but less time per unit of resource, the rate of procurement increasing with more procurement—as would happen, for example, if procurement provided information about resource distribution, increasing what might be called its "effective concentration" and thereby improving foraging efficiency. By similar reasoning, setting $e < 0$ implies that procuring the larger amount needed for a processed load will take more time per unit of resource than will procuring the smaller amount. In this case the rate of procurement decreases, as might happen if procurement depleted a resource or made prey more wary, decreasing its effective concentration. Again, all this makes sense if we think of e in relation to its effect on travel time switching point $t_{j-1\leftrightarrow j}$. The likelihood of field processing increases directly with resource concentration e.

Thus we have finally arrived at a general model of field processing applicable to virtually any resource:

$$t_{j-1\leftrightarrow j} \quad = p_j \left(u_{j-1} / [u_j - u_{j-1}] \right) - se \qquad \text{where}$$

$$e \qquad = \text{coefficient of resource concentration}$$

One very last thing before we go (I keep saying that, but this time it's true!). Remember Murphy? Remember "If anything can go wrong, it will"? Well, this is a good thing to keep in mind any time you're inclined to do something fancy with the general model of field processing. Remember Murphy any time you're tempted to assume the coefficient of resource concentration is anything other than 0 (zero). Unless you have a very good reason to assume otherwise (and solid data to back up that assumption), for most resources, most of the time, your best bet is that $e = 0$.

FURTHER READING

Bettinger, R. L., R. Malhi, and H. McCarthy. (1997). Central Place Models of Acorn and Mussel Processing. *Journal of Archaeological Science* 24:887–899.

The original publication of the field processing model described in this chapter.

EXERCISES FOR CHAPTER 5

5.1. For the cases described in Table 5.3, calculate critical travel time switching point $t_{j-1\leftrightarrow j}$ at which processing and not processing produce the same rate of return. Assume $e = 0$.

5.2. Table 5.4 describes a resource processing problem in which stage j has two substages ja and jb. Table 5.4 shows the utilities and processing times for the two substages but not for stage j as a whole.

Table 5.3. Data for Exercise 5.1

Case	Processing hr p_j	Utility before processing u_{j-1}	Utility after processing u_j	Travel time switching point (hr) $t_{j-1 \leftrightarrow j}$
1	25.00	.10	1.00	
2	3.00	.36	.75	
3	100.00	99 kg	100 kg	
4	5.70	$400	$600	
5	2.30	239 kcal	400 kcal	
6	3.00	1 biface unit	2 biface units	
7	7.00	5 oz/ton	10 oz/ton	
8	6.10	.33	.30	

5.2A. Calculate utility and total processing time for stage j.

5.2B. Use the values for utility and total processing time that you obtained for stage j to obtain $t_{j-1 \leftrightarrow j}$, the critical roundtrip travel time above which processing to stage j produces higher returns.

5.3. Table 5.5 describes a resource processing problem in which the next processing stage j consists of three substages ja, jb, jc. Table 5.5 shows the utilities and processing times for the three substages but not for stage j as a whole.

Table 5.4. Data for Exercise 5.2

	Stage $j-1$	Stage j Substage j_{1st}	Stage j Substage j_{2nd}	Stage j	$t_{j-1 \leftrightarrow j}$
Processing time (hr)	$p_{j-1} = 1$	$p_{ja} = 2$	$p_{jb} = 1$		
Utility	$u_{j-1} = .50$	$u_{ja} = .75$	$u_{jb} = .80$		—

Table 5.5. Data for Exercise 5.3

| | Stage j | | | | |
Stage j-1	Substage j_{1st}	Substage j_{2nd}	Substage j_{3rd}	Stage j	$t_{j-1 \leftrightarrow j}$
Processing time (hr) $\quad p_{j-1} = 1$	$p_{ja} = 2$	$p_{jb} = 1$	$p_{jc} = 1$		
Utility $\quad u_{j-1} = .50$	$u_{ja} = .75$	$u_{jb} = .80$	$u_{jc} = .85$		—

5.3A. Calculate utility and total processing time at stage j.

5.3B. Use the values for utility and total processing time that you obtained for stage j to obtain $t_{j-1 \leftrightarrow j}$, the critical roundtrip travel time above which processing to stage j produces higher returns.

5.4. Robert Bettinger, Ripan Malhi, and Helen McCarthy (1997; see "Further Reading") summarize the relevant times and quantities for the successive steps entailed in preparing a batch of leached acorn meal, starting with 15.90 kilograms of acorns which are successively reduced to 5.00 kilograms of meal that has been leached to remove tannic acid. These data are given in Table 5.6. Bettinger, Malhi, and McCarthy (1997) show that weight of the acorn product at any stage indexes utility (i.e., utility increases as weight decreases), reaching its maximum value (u_j = 1.00) as (pounded) meal.

Table 5.6. Data for Exercise 5.4

Stage	Activity	Weight (kg)	Min/kg	u_j	$t_{j-1 \leftrightarrow j}$ (min/kg)
1	Gather	15.90	5.32		—
2	Dry (100%)	13.00	0.55		
3	Shuck/winnow	6.50	83.15		
4	Clean	5.58	83.87		
5	Pound	5.00	82.36	1.00	
6	Leach	5.00	28.00		

5.4A. Calculate utilities for acorn at each stage.

5.4B. Use your calculated utilities and given processing times to determine the travel point switching time for each stage in minutes per kilogram. Assume $e = 0$.

ANSWERS TO CHAPTER 5 EXERCISES

5.1. Travel time switching point hr $t_{j-1\leftrightarrow j}$.

Case 1: $t_{j-1\leftrightarrow j}$ = 2.78 hr

$$= p_j\ (u_{j-1}\ /\ [u_j\ -\ u_{j-1}])$$

$$= 25.00\ (.10\ /\ [1.00\ -\ .10])$$

$$= 25.00\ (.10\ /\ .90)$$

$$= 25.00\ (.11)$$

$$= 2.78\ hr$$

Case 2 = 2.77 hr; Case 3 = 9900.00 hr; Case 4 = 11.40 hr; Case 5 = 3.41 hr; Case 6 = 3.00 hr; Case 7 = 7.00 hr; Case 8 = no answer—processing decreases utility.

5.2A. u_j = .80, p_j = 3.13 hr

p_j $= (p_{j1st}\ [u_{j2nd}\ /\ u_{j1st}])\ +\ p_{j2nd}$

$$= (2[.80\ /\ .75])\ +\ p_{j2nd}$$

$$= 2.13\ +\ p_{j2nd}$$

$$= 2.13\ +\ 1$$

$$= 3.13\ hr$$

5.2B. $t_{j-1\leftrightarrow j}$ = 5.22 hr

$$= p_j(u_{j-1}\ /\ [u_j\ -\ u_{j-1}])$$

$$= 3.13\ hr\ (u_{j-1}\ /\ [u_j\ -\ u_{j-1}])$$

$$= 3.13\ hr\ (.50\ /\ [.80\ -\ .50])$$

$$= 5.22\ hr$$

5.3A. u_j = .85, p_j = $p_{j1st\&2nd\&3rd}$ = 4.33 hr

Step 1 $p_{j1st\&2nd}$ $= p_{j1st}(u_{j2nd} / u_{j1st}) + p_{j2nd}$

$= 2.00(.80 / .75) + 1$

$= 2.13 + 1$

$= 3.13$ hr

Step 2 $p_{j1st\&2nd\&3rd}$ $= p_{j1st\&2nd}(u_{j3rd} / u_{j2nd}) + p_{j3rd}$

$= 3.13(.85 / .80) + 1$

$= 3.33 + 1$

$= 4.33$ hr

5.3B. $t_{j-1\leftrightarrow j}$ $= 6.19$ hr

$= p_j(u_{j-1} / [u_j - u_{j-1}])$

$= 4.33 \ (.50 / [.85 - .50])$

$= 6.19$ hr

5.4A.   Utility: Stage 1 = .31

u_{stage1} $= u_{stage5}(wt_{stage5} / wt_{stage1})$

$= 1.00(5.00 \text{ kg} / 15.90 \text{ kg})$

$= 5.00 \text{ kg} / 15.90 \text{ kg}$

$= .31$

Stage 2 = .38; Stage 3 = .77; Stage 4 = .90; Stage 5 = 1.00; Stage 6 = 1.00.

5.4B. Travel time switching point (min/kg): Stage 1 = not applicable; Stage 2 = 2.47; Stage 3 = 83.15; Stage 4 = 508.69; Stage 5 = 710.00; Stage 6 = none — processing does not increase utility; leaching will never be done in the field (nor will cooking for that matter). Rounding error accounts for the differences between these answers and the values shown by Bettinger, Malhi, and McCarthy (1997).

APPENDICES

APPENDIX 1: VARIABLES USED

a Slope of line plotted in X,Y coordinates: change in Y as a function of change in X (Chapter 2).

b Y-intercept: Y-axis intercept of any line plotted in X,Y coordinates (Chapter 2).

c Culinary time: time needed to prepare a stored resource for final consumption (Chapter 3).

d Deferred cost: cost of an activity i that may not have to be performed (Chapter 3).

e Coefficient of resource concentration (Chapter 5).

f Foraging time: time expended obtaining and processing a resource (Chapter 4).

i Initial cost: cost of an activity that must be performed (Chapter 3).

m Manufacturing time: time spent making a procurement technology (Chapter 4).

p Processing time: time required to process a load to a particular condition or stage (Chapter 5).

q Probability of a cache being used (Chapter 3).

r Procurement rate: rate (kcal/hr) at which a resource is obtained using a given technology (Chapter 4).

s Procurement time: time expended procuring a resource (Chapters 4, 5).

t Travel time: time spent traveling to and from foraging location— that is, roundtrip. (Chapters 4, 5).

u Utility: value of a resource (Chapters 4, 5).

z Storage time: time required to acquire and process a resource for storage (Chapter 3).

APPENDIX 2: LINEAR PROGRAMMING
(CHAPTER 2)

Solving for the intersection of two constraint lines:

Constraint 1	Y	$=$	$a_1X + b_1$
Constraint 2	Y	$=$	$a_2X + b_2$
Begin	$a_1X + b_1$	$=$	$a_2X + b_2$
Subtract b_1	a_1X	$=$	$a_2X + b_2 - b_1$
Subtract a_2X	$a_1X - a_2X$	$=$	$b_2 - b_1$
Factor left term	$X(a_1 - a_2)$	$=$	$b_2 - b_1$
Divide by $(a_1 - a_2)$	X	$=$	$(b_2 - b_1) / (a_1 - a_2)$
Done!	X	$=$	$(b_2 - b_1) / (a_1 - a_2)$

APPENDIX 3: FRONT-BACK LOADED RESOURCE MODEL
(CHAPTER 3)

Solving for q in the equation:

$$q(z_1 + c_1) + (1 - q)z_1 = q(z_2 + c_2) + (1 - q)z_2$$

I solved the equation this way:

Start	$q(z_1 + c_1) + (1 - q)z_1$	$=$	$q(z_2 + c_2) + (1 - q)z_2$
Expand terms on both sides	$qz_1 + qc_1 + z_1 - qz_1$	$=$	$qz_2 + qc_2 + z_2 - qz_2$
Gather like terms	$qz_1 - qz_1 + qc_1 + z_1$	$=$	$qz_2 - qz_2 + qc_2 + z_2$
Cancel terms	$qc_1 + z_1$	$=$	$qc_2 + z_2$
Subtract qc_2	$qc_1 + z_1 - qc_2$	$=$	z_2
Subtract z_1	$qc_1 - qc_2$	$=$	$z_2 - z_1$
Factor left side	$q(c_1 - c_2)$	$=$	$z_2 - z_1$

| Divide by $c_1 - c_2$ | q | $=$ | $(z_2 - z_1) / (c_1 - c_2)$ |
| Done! | q | $=$ | $(z_2 - z_1) / (c_1 - c_2)$ |

APPENDIX 4: TECHNOLOGICAL INVESTMENT MODEL (CHAPTER 4)

Solving for s in the equation:

$$r_2 / (m_2 + s) = r_1 / (m_1 + s)$$

There are probably many ways to go at this, but this one works:

Start	$r_2 / (m_2 + s)$	$=$	$r_1 / (m_1 + s)$
Multiply by $(m_2 + s)$	r_2	$=$	$(m_2 + s)r_1 / (m_1 + s)$
Multiply by $(m_1 + s)$	$r_2(m_1 + s)$	$=$	$r_1(m_2 + s)$
Expand both sides	$r_2 m_1 + r_2 s$	$=$	$r_1 m_2 + r_1 s$
Subtract $r_1 s$	$r_2 m_1 + r_2 s - r_1 s$	$=$	$r_1 m_2$
Factor left side	$r_2 m_1 + s(r_2 - r_1)$	$=$	$r_1 m_2$
Subtract $r_2 m_1$	$s(r_2 - r_1)$	$=$	$r_1 m_2 - r_2 m_1$
Divide by $(r_2 - r_1)$	s	$=$	$(r_1 m_2 - r_2 m_1) / (r_2 - r_1)$
Done!	s	$=$	$(r_1 m_2 - r_2 m_1) / (r_2 - r_1)$

APPENDIX 5: GENERIC FIELD PROCESSING MODEL (CHAPTER 4)

Solving for t in the equation:

$$u_2 / (f_2 + t) = u_1 / (f_1 + t)$$

Begin	$u_2 / (f_2 + t)$	$=$	$u_1 / (f_1 + t)$
Multiply by $(f_2 + t)$	u_2	$=$	$(f_2 + t)u_1 / (f_1 + t)$
Multiply by $(f_1 + t)$	$u_2(f_1 + t)$	$=$	$u_1(f_2 + t)$
Expand both sides	$u_2 f_1 + u_2 t$	$=$	$u_1 f_2 + u_1 t$

Subtract u_1t	$u_2f_1 + u_2t - u_1t$	$=$	u_1f_2
Factor left side	$u_2f_1 + t(u_2 - u_1)$	$=$	u_1f_2
Subtract u_2f_1	$t(u_2 - u_1)$	$=$	$u_1f_2 - u_2f_1$
Divide by $(u_2 - u_1)$	t	$=$	$(u_1f_2 - u_2f_1) / (u_2 - u_1)$
Done!	t	$=$	$(u_1f_2 - u_2f_1) / (u_2 - u_1)$

APPENDIX 6: FIELD PROCESSING (CHAPTER 5)

Table A.1 furnishes quantitative values for the example depicted in Figure 5.2, where a load of nuts must fit in a 1 x 1 square and its equivalent in three dimensions, a 1 x 1 x 1 cube. The key idea is that processing that increases utility increases time required for all prior stages directly in proportion to the utility after processing relative to the utility before processing. Thus, in the two-dimensional case, if 4 units of procurement time are

Table A.1. Data for Figure 5.2

	2 dimensions			3 dimensions			
Item state	Whole	Husked	Shelled	Item state	Whole	Husked	Shelled
Item diameter	0.500	0.333	0.250	Item diameter	0.500	0.333	0.250
Total items	4	9	16	Total items	8	27	64
Item area	0.196	0.087	0.049	Item volume	0.065	0.019	0.008
Item utility	0.250	0.563	1.000	Item utility	0.125	0.422	1.000
Total item area	0.785	0.785	0.785	Total item volume	0.524	0.524	0.524
Total utility	0.196	0.442	0.785	Total utility	0.065	0.221	0.524
Load type	Whole	Husked	Shelled	Load type	Whole	Husked	Shelled
Procure	4 items	9 items	16 items	Procure	8 items	27 items	64 items
Husk		9 items	16 items	Husk		27 items	64 items
Shell			16 items	Shell			64 items

required to obtain a full load of unprocessed nuts whose utility is 19.6%, 9 units of procurement time will be required if husks are removed to obtain a full load whose utility is 44.2% (4 x 44.2 / 19.6 = 9). Similarly, in the three-dimensional case, if 8 units of procurement time are required to obtain a full load of unprocessed nuts whose utility is 6.5%, 27 units of procurement time will be required if husks are removed to obtain a full load whose utility is 22.1% (8 x 22.1 / 6.5 = 27). The values shown are subject to rounding error.

APPENDIX 7: FIELD PROCESSING (CHAPTER 5)

Solving for t in the equation:

$$u_j / (s_j + p_j + t) = u_{j-1} / (s_{j-1} + t)$$

Again, there are probably many ways to solve this, but this one works. The trick is the substitution in the very first step. As explained in Chapter 5, the relationship between procurement time with processing s_j and procurement time without processing s_{j-1} is a function of the relationship of utility with processing u_j and utility without processing u_{j-1} — specifically $s_j / s_{j-1} = u_j / u_{j-1}$, which when rearranged gives $s_j = s_{j-1}(u_j / u_{j-1})$, the term substituted in the first step.

Start	$u_j / (s_j + p_j + t)$	$=$	$u_{j-1} / (s_{j-1} + t)$
Substitute $[s_{j-1}u_j / u_{j-1}]$ for s_j	$u_j / ([s_{j-1}u_j / u_{j-1}] + p_j + t)$	$=$	$u_{j-1} / (s_{j-1} + t)$
Multiply by $([s_{j-1}u_j / u_{j-1}] + p_j + t)$	u_j	$=$	$([\{s_{j-1}u_j / u_{j-1}\} + p_j + t]u_{j-1}) / (s_{j-1} + t)$
Expand right term	u_j	$=$	$(s_{j-1}u_j + p_ju_{j-1} + tu_{j-1}) / (s_{j-1} + t)$
Multiply by $(s_{j-1} + t)$	$u_j(s_{j-1} + t)$	$=$	$s_{j-1}u_j + p_ju_{j-1} + tu_{j-1}$
Expand left term	$s_{j-1}u_j + tu_j$	$=$	$s_{j-1}u_j + p_ju_{j-1} + tu_{j-1}$
Subtract $s_{j-1}u_j$	tu_j	$=$	$p_ju_{j-1} + tu_{j-1}$
Subtract tu_{j-1}	$tu_j - tu_{j-1}$	$=$	p_ju_{j-1}

Factor left term	$t(u_j - u_{j-1})$	$=$	$p_j u_{j-1}$
Divide by $(u_j - u_{j-1})$	t	$=$	$p_j u_{j-1} / (u_j - u_{j-1})$
Done!	t	$=$	$p_j(u_{j-1} / [u_j - u_{j-1}])$

APPENDIX 8: BIG PACKAGE FIELD PROCESSING (CHAPTER 5)

Solving for t in the equation:

$$u_j / (s + p_{j-1}[u_j / u_{j-1}] + p_j + t) = u_{j-1} / (s + p_{j-1} + t)$$

The terms here include:

t	Travel time at which processing to stage j and processing only to the prior stage j-1 produce equivalent return rates.
s	Procurement time.
u_j	Utility at stage j.
u_{j-1}	Utility at stage j-1.
p_j	Processing time at stage j when a load is processed to stage j.
p_{j-1}	Processing time at stage j-1 when a load is processed to stage j-1.
$p_{j-1}(u_j / u_{j-1})$	Processing time at stage j-1 when a load is processed to stage j.

The only tricky term here is $p_{j-1}(u_j / u_{j-1})$, which is processing time that must be spent at stage j-1 when a load is processed to stage j. As explained in the text, just as in small package processing, when big packages are processed, each successive stage of processing increases the time that must be spent in prior stages of processing as a function of utility after the final stage of processing u_j relative to utility immediately before final processing u_{j-1}. This does *not* extend to procurement time s because procurement time does not change when big package resources are processed, this being the property that defines big packages, distinguishing them from small packages.

Start	$u_j / (s + p_{j-1}[u_j / u_{j-1}] + p_j + t)$	$=$	$u_{j-1} / (s + p_{j-1} + t)$
Multiply by $(s + p_{j-1}[u_j / u_{j-1}] + p_j + t)$	u_j	$=$	$(u_{j-1})(s + p_{j-1}[u_j / u_{j1}] + p_j + t) / s + p_j + t$
Multiply by $(s + p_{j-1} + t)$	$u_j (s + p_{j-1} + t)$	$=$	$(u_{j-1})(s + p_{j-1}[u_j / u_{j-1}] + p_j + t)$
Expand terms on both sides	$u_j s + u_j p_{j-1} + u_j t$	$=$	$u_{j-1} s + u_j p_{j-1} + u_{j-1} p_j + u_{j-1} t$
Cancel terms, i.e., $u_j p_{j-1}$	$u_j s + u_j t$	$=$	$u_{j-1} s + u_{j-1} p_j + u_{j-1} t$
Factor terms on both sides	$u_j(s + t)$	$=$	$u_{j-1}(s + t) + u_{j-1} p_j$
Subtract $u_{j-1}(s + t)$	$u_j(s + t) - u_{j-1}(s + t)$	$=$	$u_{j-1} p_j$
Factor left side	$(u_j - u_{j-1})(s + t)$	$=$	$u_{j-1} p_j$
Divide by $(u_j - u_{j-1})$	$s + t$	$=$	$(u_{j-1} p_j) / (u_j - u_{j-1})$
Rearrange right side	$s + t$	$=$	$p_j (u_{j-1} / [u_j - u_{j-1}])$
Subtract s	t	$=$	$p_j (u_{j-1} / [u_j - u_{j-1}]) - s$
Done!	$t_{j-1 \leftrightarrow j}$	$=$	$p_j (u_{j-1} / [u_j - u_{j-1}]) - s$